INTERDEPENDENCE RELATIONSHIPS

Break Free from Codependency and Build Deep, Healthy Love Without Losing Yourself

by

DR. RACHEL LYMAN

Copyright 2025 Dr. Rachel Lyman. All rights reserved.

No part of this book may be reproduced in any form or by any electronic or mechanical means including information storage and retrieval systems, without permission in writing from the author. The only exception is by a reviewer, who may quote short excerpts in a review.

Although the author and publisher have made every effort to ensure that the information in this book was correct at press time, the author and publisher do not assume and hereby disclaim any liability to any party for any loss, damage, or disruption caused by errors or omissions, whether such errors or omissions result from negligence, accident, or any other cause.

This publication is designed to provide accurate and authoritative information with regard to the subject matter covered. It is sold with the understanding that the publisher is not engaged in rendering professional services. If legal advice or other expert assistance is required, the services of a competent professional should be sought.

The fact that an organization or website is referred to in this work as a citation and/or a potential source of further information does not mean that the author or the publisher endorses the information the organization or website may provide or recommendations it may make.

Please remember that Internet websites listed in this work may have changed or disappeared between when this work was written and when it is read.

Interdependence Relationships : Break Free from Codependency and Build Deep, Healthy Love Without Losing Yourself

TABLE OF CONTENTS

UNDERSTANDING INTERDEPENDENCE AND CODEPENDENCY 9

CHAPTER 1 15
What Is Codependency—Really?

CHAPTER 2 27
Where It All Begins: Childhood Wounds and Attachment Styles

CHAPTER 3 39
The Cycle of Codependent Relationships

CHAPTER 4 51
Red Flags in Toxic Partnerships

CHAPTER 5 63
The First Step—Building Self-Awareness

CHAPTER 6 75
SETTING BOUNDARIES WITHOUT GUILT

CHAPTER 7 85
THE POWER OF SELF-WORTH IN HEALING

CHAPTER 8 95
FROM REACTIVITY TO RESPONSE IN
RELATIONSHIPS

CHAPTER 9 107
WHAT INTERDEPENDENCE LOOKS LIKE IN
PRACTICE

CHAPTER 10 121
COMMUNICATION THAT DEEPENS INTIMACY

CHAPTER 11 133
LOVING WITHOUT LOSING YOURSELF

CHAPTER 12 145
WHEN THEY DON'T WANT TO CHANGE

CHAPTER 13 157
DATING AFTER CODEPENDENCY

CHAPTER 14 .... **169**
LIVING AUTHENTICALLY IN ALL RELATIONSHIPS

CHAPTER 15 .... **179**
YOUR RELATIONSHIP WITH YOURSELF

CHAPTER 16 .... **191**
REBUILDING TRUST IN YOURSELF AND OTHERS

CHAPTER 17 .... **201**
DEVELOPING EMOTIONAL RESILIENCE

CHAPTER 18 .... **213**
CULTIVATING MUTUAL RESPECT IN PARTNERSHIPS

CHAPTER 19 .... **225**
NAVIGATING INTIMACY WITH CONFIDENCE

CHAPTER 20 .... **235**
HEALING THROUGH FORGIVENESS

CHAPTER 21 .... **247**
SELF-CARE STRATEGIES FOR RELATIONSHIP HEALTH

CHAPTER 22 .... **257**
EMBRACING INDEPENDENCE WITHIN TOGETHERNESS

CHAPTER 23 .... **269**
RECOGNIZING AND AVOIDING RELAPSE TRIGGERS

CHAPTER 24 .... **279**
CREATING A VISION FOR YOUR RELATIONSHIP FUTURE

CHAPTER 25 .... **291**
BECOMING AN ADVOCATE FOR HEALTHY RELATIONSHIPS

EMBRACING INTERDEPENDENCE AS A LIFELONG JOURNEY **302**

APPENDIX: TOOLS AND RESOURCES FOR CONTINUED GROWTH **307**

UNDERSTANDING INTERDEPENDENCE AND CODEPENDENCY

Relationships can be some of the most enriching and challenging parts of life. At their best, they offer connection, support, and growth; at their worst, they can trap us in unhealthy patterns that drain our energy and sense of self. Two concepts central to navigating relationships well are interdependence and codependency. While they sound similar and often get confused, they represent very different dynamics, with vastly different effects on our emotional well-being. Understanding the distinction is the first step toward building healthier, more fulfilling bonds with those around us.

Codependency is often described as an excessive emotional or psychological reliance on another person, typically one who requires support due to illness or addiction. But this definition barely scratches the surface. More broadly, codependency is a pattern where a person sacrifices their own needs to fulfill someone else's, often losing sight of their identity along the way. This pattern can sneak into romantic relationships, friendships, and family ties, leading to imbalance and emotional exhaustion. It usually thrives on fear—the fear of abandonment, rejection, or being alone. Over time, these fears manifest as controlling behaviors, people-pleasing, or an inability to set boundaries.

Interdependence, by contrast, is built on mutual respect, trust, and emotional responsibility. It's the recognition that while each partner maintains their own individuality and autonomy, they can rely on each other in healthy and supportive ways. Interdependent relationships celebrate two whole people coming together—not to complete each other, but to complement and empower one another. This kind of bond nurtures growth rather than enforces dependence.

The journey from codependency toward interdependence is rarely straightforward, but it's one filled with profound breakthroughs and renewed hope. For many, the cycle of codependent behavior feels like a trap—one that's hard to detect at first because the desire to care deeply and be close is natural. However, when that desire turns into emotional fusion or a loss of boundaries, it sets the stage for recurring pain and frustration. This book aims to guide you gently through understanding these patterns, shining light on what's happening beneath the surface of your relationships.

Why does it matter so much to recognize codependency early on? Because without awareness, unhealthy patterns tend to repeat themselves, leaving people stuck in a cycle of emotional sacrifice and unmet needs. When you don't know how to maintain a sense of self while caring for someone else, relationships can feel like a constant balancing act on shaky ground. This imbalance affects not just emotional health but also physical well-being, career choices, and overall life satisfaction. Interdependence offers an alternative model—one where connection and autonomy coexist, allowing love to flourish without losing yourself in the process.

It's important to emphasize that interdependence is not about dependence or independence in isolation. Independence suggests going it alone, while dependence implies a one-sided reliance that can become unhealthy. Interdependence finds the middle ground—a dance between giving and receiving, vulnerability and strength. It requires both partners to show up authentically while respecting each other's boundaries and personal growth. This balance supports emotional resilience, fosters genuine intimacy, and prevents the burnout so common in codependent relationships.

Many factors feed into our tendency to develop codependent behaviors. Early life experiences, especially childhood attachments, shape how we connect with others as adults. While this book will dive deeper into those roots later, it's enough for now to acknowledge that understanding your personal history is a vital step toward healing. Recognizing the origins of your relationship patterns helps demystify behaviors that might have felt confusing or shameful. It also opens the door to developing new ways of relating that nurture rather than deplete you.

The road ahead will also challenge some common myths around love and care. For example, many people believe that "love means sacrifice" or that "if someone really loves you, they'll accept you no matter what." These beliefs can be damaging when taken to extremes. True love does involve compromise but not at the cost of losing your own voice or well-being. Acceptance doesn't mean tolerating disrespect or neglect. Separating love from sacrifice in unhealthy ways is liberating and necessary for developing balanced relationships.

Taking this journey involves building a toolkit that includes self-awareness, boundary-setting, and communication skills. Without these tools, it's easy to fall back into familiar but harmful codependent patterns. This isn't about blaming yourself or others but about empowerment—knowing what you need, valuing yourself, and learning how to ask for what you deserve. The shift toward interdependence calls for courage and commitment to change old habits and embrace new possibilities.

This guide is designed for anyone who feels caught in a web of emotional dependency or who longs for relationships that uplift and sustain them. Whether you're recovering from a codependent relationship or simply want to deepen your current connections, the principles here provide a roadmap. They encourage reflection without judgment and growth without pressure. As you move through the chapters, you'll discover practical exercises, thought-provoking insights, and strategies grounded in empathy and respect. The goal is to help you take meaningful steps toward freedom and wholeness.

Healing from codependency isn't about quick fixes or overnight transformations. It's a process—a lifelong practice of cultivating healthy habits, making conscious choices, and showing up for yourself and loved ones in new, loving ways. This process doesn't mean you'll never face challenges or moments of doubt. Instead, it offers a foundation to navigate those difficulties with greater clarity and strength. It's about becoming emotionally resilient and creating relationships that bring joy instead of pain.

Ultimately, understanding the difference between interdependence and codependency empowers you to make informed choices in your relationships. It allows you to identify when you're slipping into old patterns and provides the tools to course-correct. You'll learn how to balance intimacy with independence and care with self-respect. This balance opens the way to connections that reflect your true needs and values, creating space for deeper love and connection.

As you begin this exploration, remember that change takes time and patience. The willingness to reflect honestly and try new ways of relating is a powerful act of self-love. Each step forward, no matter how small, moves you closer to healthier, more balanced relationships filled with mutual respect, trust, and compassion. By understanding interdependence and codependency, you hold the key to breaking free from limiting patterns and embracing relationships that support your personal growth and emotional well-being.

CHAPTER 1

WHAT IS CODEPENDENCY—
REALLY?

Codependency often gets misunderstood as simply being overly "nice" or "helpful," but it's much more complex than these surface ideas suggest. At its core, codependency involves a deep pattern where a person's sense of self becomes entangled with another's needs or emotions to the point of losing personal boundaries and autonomy. It's not just about sacrifice; it's about an imbalanced relationship dynamic where one's own well-being takes a backseat to maintaining connection or approval, often driven by fear of abandonment or conflict. Many people struggling with codependency don't realize they're caught in a loop of seeking validation through caretaking, which can lead to exhaustion and emotional confusion. Understanding what codependency really entails is the first step toward breaking free from these unhealthy patterns and building relationships based on mutual respect, self-awareness, and emotional resilience.

Common Myths and Misconceptions About Codependency

When people hear the term "codependency," a lot of preconceived ideas rush in, many of which miss the mark or oversimplify what it really means. These myths can keep someone stuck, feeling shame or confusion instead of moving toward healing and healthier relationships. That's why it's essential to unravel some of the most common misunderstandings about codependency before diving deeper into recognizing it and making meaningful changes.

One widespread myth is that codependency is just about being "too nice" or "a people-pleaser." Sure, those traits can be part of it, but codependency runs much deeper than occasional kindness or wanting to maintain peace. It's less about surface behaviors and more about an internal pattern where a person's sense of worth, identity, and emotional safety become intertwined with taking care of someone else—often to the point of self-neglect. So codependency isn't simply being kind; it's a complex emotional trap where love, fear, and a need for control all intermingle.

Some people think codependency only shows up in romantic relationships. That's a big misconception, too. While it often appears most glaringly in romantic partnerships, codependency can exist in any close connection—family, friendships, or even work dynamics. The common thread is that the individual loses a clear grip on where their emotional experience ends and the other's begins. This blurring fuels unhealthy dependence and can happen with anyone we feel responsible for or connected to closely.

Another myth to clear up is the idea that codependency is a character flaw or moral weakness. Nothing could be farther from the truth. It's a learned coping mechanism, usually developed in response to difficult early environments or relational wounds. Many who struggle with codependency grew up in families where emotional needs were inconsistently met or blurred with obligation and caretaking roles. Recognizing this helps shift away from blame and toward curiosity and compassion about why these patterns began.

Over time, this misunderstanding can make people label themselves as "broken" or "too much" simply because they struggle to set boundaries or say no. But codependency isn't about lack of willpower. It's about deep-seated fears of abandonment, rejection, or chaos that push someone to overfunction or accommodate others excessively. Healing begins when those fears are acknowledged, not condemned.

Another common misconception is that codependency always involves dramatic dysfunction or abuse. While it can accompany toxic or harmful relationships, codependency itself is more subtle and often invisible to outsiders. You might know someone quietly putting their needs last, constantly worriting about pleasing others, or suppressing emotions to avoid conflict. These behaviors don't always scream "problem" in the traditional sense, but they slowly erode self-esteem and emotional well-being.

There's also a false belief that codependency is permanent or impossible to overcome. Some think once someone is "codependent," they're stuck with it forever. That's simply not true. Codependency is a pattern, not a destiny. With consistent self-awareness, healthy practice, and often support, people can reclaim their autonomy and build much stronger, balanced connections. The key is recognizing the behavior and understanding what's driving it, rather than feeling trapped by it.

Many confuse codependency with love or commitment. They believe that being codependent means caring too much or loving too deeply. But healthy love thrives on mutual respect, balance, and the freedom to be yourself—even when things get tough. Codependency, on the other hand, thrives on fear-driven actions that prioritize another's needs over your own well-being. It's important to distinguish unconditional love from over-responsibility masked as care.

People sometimes think that setting boundaries in codependent relationships means being selfish or uncaring. The truth is exactly the opposite. Boundaries are acts of self-love that protect your emotional health and help create clearer, more respectful relationships. Without boundaries, codependency grows in the shadows of guilt, obligation, and blurred identities. Reinforcing boundaries doesn't mean you love less; it means you love better—for yourself and for others.

Another myth to challenge is the assumption that codependency is always obvious to the person living it. Many don't realize they're caught in these patterns because codependency can be normalized in families and cultures. If you grew up in an environment where taking care of others at the expense of yourself was praised or expected, these behaviors might feel like natural expressions of love. That normalization makes it harder to spot the difference between healthy care and detrimental dependence.

Some also believe you can't have fulfilling relationships if you have codependent tendencies. The good news is that learning about codependency is the first step toward rewiring those patterns. The journey toward interdependence involves growing the capacity to give and receive love healthily, recognizing personal limits, and developing emotional resilience. Fulfillment in relationships is absolutely possible when you understand codependency rather than letting it define you.

It's easy to fall into the trap of thinking codependency means doing too much for others physically—like always running errands, fixing problems, or managing someone else's responsibilities. While these external actions matter, codependency is more about what happens emotionally underneath. It's the feeling that your value depends on how much you sacrifice or control, rather than a balance between your needs and the other person's.

Finally, some think that simply stopping caretaking behaviors will break codependency. But without addressing the emotional fears and beliefs underneath, this often leads to guilt, confusion, or relapse. True change comes from working through the internal codependent scripts, learning to sit with discomfort, and building a solid sense of self-worth that isn't dependent on others' approval or stability.

By peeling back these myths, it becomes clear that codependency is a multifaceted experience rooted in emotional complexity rather than just bad habits or selfishness. Understanding these misconceptions helps you move toward greater clarity and compassion—for yourself and others—and lays an important foundation for building resilient, interdependent relationships. Once you see codependency not as a personal failure but as a pattern shaped by experience, you open the door to freedom and lasting change.

Signs You May Be Experiencing Codependency

Recognizing codependency in your life isn't always straightforward. Often, the lines blur between caring for others and losing yourself in the process. Many people only realize they've been caught in codependent patterns once the emotional toll becomes overwhelming. So what does it feel like when these patterns are at play? What subtle and not-so-subtle signs might show up, signaling that your emotional well-being is deeply entangled with someone else's needs or approval?

One common sign is an overwhelming need to please others to feel worthy or accepted. If you frequently put other people's desires above your own, even when it leads to personal discomfort or dissatisfaction, this tendency might be more than just generosity. It's a red flag pointing towards codependency. You might find yourself feeling anxious or guilty if you say no or set clear boundaries. This internal discomfort often pushes people to accommodate others repeatedly, often at great personal expense.

Closely tied to this is difficulty in identifying or expressing your own feelings and needs. When you constantly tune into what others want or expect, your own emotions can get muffled or ignored. You may struggle to articulate what you want out of a relationship—or even confuse your own feelings with those of your partner or family member. This blurring can make it hard to distinguish where you end and someone else begins emotionally. Over time, this leads to a loss of personal identity and confusion about your own values and priorities.

Another sign is an intense fear of abandonment or rejection. Whether this fear is rooted in past experiences or current insecurities, it can drive codependent behavior. You might notice feeling desperate to keep people close, often excusing neglect, disrespect, or even manipulation to avoid being alone. This fear fuels what some call "emotional fusion," where your happiness feels completely dependent on the approval or presence of another. The internal message tends to be, "If they leave me, I am nothing."

It's not unusual for codependent individuals to experience chronic low self-esteem. They often believe they are unworthy of love unless they're indispensable to someone else. This belief can lead to compulsive caretaking behaviors, where taking care of others becomes a way to earn value or avoid feeling empty inside. When self-worth is tied to usefulness, it's challenging to rest, relax, and accept unconditional love—because it feels unfamiliar or unsafe.

Many people caught in codependency report feeling a persistent sense of responsibility for other people's feelings and problems. They may habitually try to "fix" others, often overextending themselves emotionally and physically. This caretaking role offers a sense of purpose but can drain energy and deepen exhaustion. Meanwhile, the person may neglect their own needs or avoid facing their challenges because they focus so much on others. Sometimes, these caretakers silently hope that their efforts will eventually be reciprocated, but all too often, that expectation remains unmet.

Another revealing sign involves difficulty setting and maintaining healthy boundaries. Boundaries are crucial for balanced relationships, but for someone experiencing codependency, the very idea of saying no or putting limits on what they'll tolerate can trigger guilt or anxiety. They might allow behaviors that feel disrespectful or harmful, convincing themselves it's "just part of loving" or "being loyal." Over time, these blurred boundaries create patterns where the codependent person feels used or resentful, yet struggles to assert themselves effectively.

It's also common to see people stuck in codependent dynamics struggle with approval-seeking and fear of criticism. Feedback, even when constructive, can feel like personal rejection. They may adapt their behavior in an attempt to avoid conflict or maintain peace, which sometimes looks like walking on eggshells. This hyper-vigilance toward others' emotions often comes at the expense of authentic self-expression. The constant need for validation can wear a person down, making them feel fragile and overly dependent on external reassurance.

Codependency doesn't just affect romantic relationships; it often shows up in friendships and family connections, too. You might notice patterns where you're the one who always compromises or sacrifices, while others expect your support without reciprocating. Sometimes these relationships feel one-sided or draining, leaving you emotionally depleted but afraid to step back out of loyalty or guilt. This makes it hard to build the kind of mutual, balanced bonds that nurture personal growth and joy.

Emotional caretaking can often coincide with avoidance of personal feelings, especially difficult ones like anger or sadness. Codependent individuals tend to suppress or minimize their own emotions because addressing them feels risky or selfish. Instead, they redirect focus onto the other person's feelings or problems. This avoidance keeps the emotional system running on someone else's terms, preventing honest self-reflection and growth. Over time, this denies the codependent person crucial opportunities to heal and develop resilience.

At times, codependency shows up as repetitive relationship patterns, where the same dynamics play out across different partnerships. These might include being involved with emotionally unavailable partners, tolerating dishonesty, or accepting abuse. Despite pain and disappointment, the urge to "fix" or "save" the other person remains strong. This cycle can be confusing and painful to break because it's tied not just to behavior but to deep-rooted beliefs about love and worthiness.

It's important to recognize that these signs don't mean you're broken or doomed to unhealthy relationships forever. Awareness is the first step to change. When you notice a pattern of sacrificing your needs, struggling to say no, or fearing rejection to an unhealthy degree, you're beginning to identify areas where growth is possible. These are the moments when you can gently challenge old habits and open space to reclaim your sense of self.

Signs of codependency can feel heavy or uncomfortable to face. Still, understanding these patterns offers powerful motivation to seek healthier ways of connecting. It can spark a longing for relationships where both partners feel valued, heard, and free to be themselves. Recognizing codependency is about reclaiming your emotional sovereignty—not isolating yourself, but instead learning how to love without losing who you are.

In the next chapters, we'll explore the roots of these patterns and practical steps to create balance, set boundaries, and build self-worth. But for now, notice where you see these signs in your life or relationships. Its gentle exploration allows you to start moving away from old cycles and toward a more fulfilling and interdependent way of relating. Remember, codependency doesn't define you; it's just a pattern you can change with intention and support.

CHAPTER 2

WHERE IT ALL BEGINS: CHILDHOOD WOUNDS AND ATTACHMENT STYLES

Our earliest bonds with caregivers lay the groundwork for how we'll relate to others later in life, especially when it comes to love and connection. Childhood wounds often shape the invisible script we follow in relationships, influencing whether we seek closeness or keep people at arm's length. Attachment styles—patterns formed by our experiences of safety, trust, and care—don't just appear out of nowhere; they develop through those first emotional exchanges and leave lasting impressions on our hearts. Understanding these roots helps you shed blame and opens a path toward healthier, more balanced connections by recognizing the old stories that no longer serve you. This awareness is the first step in breaking free from unhealthy cycles and moving toward the kind of interdependent relationships that truly nourish and empower both partners.

The Roots of Emotional Dependency in Childhood

It all starts early. From the moment we're born, our emotional landscape begins to take shape, influenced heavily by the care—or lack thereof—that we receive. Emotional dependency often has its roots in childhood, where the seeds of attachment are first planted. When a child's emotional needs go unmet or are inconsistently met, it fosters a deep-seated yearning for love and approval that can carry over into adult relationships in unhealthy ways. This dependency doesn't just happen overnight; it's the byproduct of patterns ingrained through interactions with primary caregivers, typically parents or guardians.

Children are wired to seek connection and security from those who care for them. When a child experiences responsive and reliable caregiving, they tend to develop a secure attachment style—a solid foundation upon which self-esteem and emotional resilience grow. Conversely, when caregiving is spotty, neglectful, or overly controlling, children learn early on that their worth may depend on earning affection or meeting others' needs. This early message plants the idea that love is conditional, making emotional dependency a way to cope with uncertainty and fear of abandonment.

Consider a child whose emotional expressions are routinely dismissed or punished. Over time, this child might suppress their feelings or constantly seek reassurance, desperate to avoid rejection. Because their internal sense of safety is unstable, they may grow into adults who struggle to distinguish their own emotional needs from others'. This blurring leads to patterns where they prioritize the feelings and approval of partners or friends over their own well-being. The origins of this dynamic lie in those formative years when a child believes their value depends on pleasing others.

Another significant factor in emotional dependency emerges from inconsistent caregiving. Imagine a parent who is loving and attentive one moment but distant and unpredictable the next. This kind of inconsistency creates confusion and anxiety. Children exposed to such fluctuating care often develop anxious attachment, characterized by heightened sensitivity to rejection and an urgent need for closeness. These children learn to stay alert, almost hypervigilant, always scanning for signs that affection might withdraw. Adults who carry this pattern forward regularly find themselves feeling clingy or overly reactive in relationships, fearing abandonment even when there's no immediate threat.

It's important to recognize that emotional dependency doesn't always stem from negative experiences alone. Even parents who genuinely want to protect their children can unintentionally foster dependency by being overly involved or controlling. When children aren't given space to develop autonomy or solve problems independently, they might internalize the belief that they're incapable of managing life on their own. This can lead to a reliance on others to regulate their emotions and make decisions—a hallmark of emotional dependency later in life.

In this sense, the roots of emotional dependency are tangled with fear—fear that love will be lost, fear that self won't be enough, and fear of abandonment. From childhood, these fears shape how individuals relate to others. When we were young, we had no choice but to depend on adults. But when that dependency doesn't transform into healthy independence, it persists, creating challenges in forming balanced, interdependent relationships as adults.

Understanding these origins is not about blaming caregivers or our past. It's about recognizing the survival strategies our younger selves developed to navigate an unpredictable world. These coping mechanisms helped us then but may limit us now. Emotional dependency often masquerades as love or loyalty, but in reality, it's a response to childhood wounds that left us feeling unsafe or unworthy.

These early emotional experiences also affect how trust is built—or broken—in relationships. Trust begins in childhood through the consistency and predictability of caregivers' responses. When trust foundations are shaky, emotional dependency can fill the void by creating an almost desperate need for reassurance. This need leads to patterns of people-pleasing, loss of boundaries, and difficulty saying "no," all attempts to keep loved ones close and affirm that one's existence matters.

Moreover, children who grow up feeling invisible or undervalued might shy away from expressing needs directly, fearing rejection. Instead, they might unconsciously use emotional dependency as a way to maintain connection by adjusting themselves, often excessively, to others' desires. This creates a cycle that can be hard to break without conscious effort and self-compassion.

Recognizing these childhood roots establishes a vital starting point for anyone committed to healing. When we see emotional dependency as a deeply ingrained response to early experiences, it becomes easier to approach personal growth with patience and kindness instead of judgment. Healing means learning to identify these old patterns, understanding their origin, and gradually cultivating a secure sense of self that doesn't rely on external validation to feel whole.

Developing this healthy sense of independence while maintaining genuine connection with others is the true goal. That balance is what interdependence looks like—relationships where two people can lean on each other without losing their individual identities. But before that transformation can occur, the roots of emotional dependency must be acknowledged and nurtured with empathy, because those roots are linked to the heart of who we were as children and shape who we become as adults.

Emotional dependency might have served as a protective shield in childhood, but it can also act like a shackle in adulthood. The journey toward emotional freedom starts with recognizing the childhood wounds that shaped our attachment needs and how those needs may have turned into dependency. From here, individuals can begin to learn new ways of relating—ways that honor both connection and autonomy.

With this understanding, we set the stage for the deeper work of reshaping attachment styles and moving toward healthier relationships. Childhood may lay the groundwork, but it doesn't define the possibilities for love and connection in adulthood. Healing those early emotional dependencies opens doors to richer, more balanced bonds that are both nurturing and empowering. This is where freedom from old patterns begins—knowing the roots can give you the strength to grow in entirely new directions.

How Early Relationships Shape Adult Love Patterns

Our earliest relationships serve as the blueprint for how we approach love and connection later in life. From infancy through childhood, the bonds we form with primary caregivers profoundly influence our expectations, behaviors, and emotional responses in adult romantic relationships. When these early connections are nurturing and consistent, they cultivate a sense of safety, trust, and emotional security. Conversely, when these bonds are inconsistent, neglectful, or even harmful, they can leave lasting wounds that ripple into adulthood.

Attachment theories give us a framework for understanding the ways childhood experiences translate directly into patterns we carry forward. Secure attachment, formed when caregivers reliably meet a child's emotional and physical needs, fosters confidence in both self and others. Adults with a secure attachment style tend to approach relationships with openness and trust, able to seek support and maintain autonomy simultaneously. On the flip side, insecure attachment styles—like anxious, avoidant, or disorganized attachment—develop when early caregiving is unpredictable or emotionally unavailable. These patterns often manifest in adult relationships through fears of abandonment, excessive dependence, or difficulties with intimacy.

It's important to recognize that these early relationship templates are not fate. They offer an explanation but don't dictate destiny. Understanding how your childhood shaped your love style can be incredibly empowering because it provides a clear starting point for healing and change. Many of the struggles in adult relationships—codependency, emotional withdrawal, or chronic dissatisfaction—have roots in unmet needs and emotional wounds carried forward from early years.

When caregivers respond to a child's needs with warmth, responsiveness, and consistent care, the child learns to view themselves as worthy of love. This feeling of worthiness forms the bedrock of healthy adult connections. On the contrary, if a caregiver dismisses, criticizes, or is intermittently available, the child's sense of worth can falter. Adult survivors of such early experiences might find themselves constantly seeking reassurance, fearing rejection, or becoming over-invested in pleasing others just to feel valued.

Patterns like these are common in codependent relationships. When emotional needs were unmet in childhood, adults may unconsciously attempt to fill that void in their romantic lives by centering their partner's needs while neglecting their own. This cycle reflects a deep-seated belief that love must be earned through sacrifice and self-neglect, often repeating the emotional exchanges experienced in early family dynamics. Recognizing this connection to childhood wounds is a vital step toward breaking free from these unbalanced patterns.

The way early caregivers handled emotional expression also shapes adult relational styles. Children who grew up in environments where vulnerability was discouraged or punished may learn to suppress their emotions, leading to difficulties with authentic emotional communication. Alternatively, those raised in chaotic or excessively enmeshed families might over-identify with others' feelings, losing boundaries and self-awareness in the process. Both extremes can stifle the natural give-and-take necessary for healthy, interdependent partnerships.

Insecure attachment patterns often create internal conflicts between the desire for closeness and the fear of losing oneself in a relationship. For example, anxious attachment triggers a deep craving for connection paired with a persistent worry about abandonment. This might lead to clinginess, jealousy, or over-monitoring a partner's behavior. Avoidant attachment, meanwhile, pushes individuals toward emotional distance and self-reliance, sometimes at the expense of intimacy and support. Neither approach supports balanced partnerships, where both individuals feel both connected and autonomous.

It's common for individuals with these early wounds to find themselves repeating an unconscious script in relationships—seeking partners who mimic the caregiving style of their childhood environment. This repetition can feel like a way to resolve the pain by trying to "get it right" this time, but often it results in replicating unhealthy dynamics. For instance, someone who experienced emotional neglect may gravitate toward unavailable partners, perpetuating feelings of loneliness and yearning. Meanwhile, someone raised with enmeshed boundaries may struggle to say no or to maintain their own identity within the relationship.

The emotional legacy of early relationships also heavily colors how adults perceive love and intimacy. Some may equate love with sacrifice, believing that enduring pain or losing themselves is proof of devotion. Others might confuse emotional distance with strength, avoiding vulnerability entirely to protect themselves from hurt. These beliefs limit the ability to engage in open, healthy partnerships and obscure the idea that love can be both supportive and freeing.

Since childhood has such a profound impact, developing awareness of these internalized patterns becomes a crucial part of cultivating healthier adult relationships. Reflecting on how you first experienced love, trust, and emotional connection can shed light on why certain relationship dynamics feel familiar—even if they're painful or unfulfilling. This awareness fosters compassion toward yourself and a readiness to address the patterns with intention and kindness rather than blame.

One powerful insight is realizing the difference between the love you experienced and the love you desire. Many adults grow up with fragmented stories of love—partial, conditional, or inconsistent—yet they carry an innocent hope for something different. Holding onto this hope fuels the motivation for change and growth, opening the door to healthier relational experiences. It's a reminder that regardless of early experiences, better connection is always possible.

However, changing these ingrained patterns demands more than just intellectual understanding. It requires emotional work and practice in real relationships—learning to set boundaries, communicate authentically, and embrace vulnerability without fear. In time, these new relational skills create alternative experiences that gradually replace old wounds. Your adult relationships can become a place where trust, respect, and mutual care thrive rather than where you replay childhood hurts.

Breaking free from the shadow of childhood attachment isn't about erasing the past, but rather integrating it into a fuller, more compassionate story of growth. By acknowledging the roots of your love patterns, you reclaim the power to rewrite the script. This process supports stepping into relationships with a balanced sense of self—strong in autonomy yet open to connection. It's where true interdependence begins, and emotional freedom takes shape.

In the journey toward healthy relationships, recognizing the role early bonds play can bring clarity and hope. They highlight not only the challenges but also the resilience present in every individual. Just as these first bonds shaped your starting point, your conscious choices can shape your relational future—moving from emotional dependency to genuine partnership where both people thrive as their authentic selves.

CHAPTER 3

THE CYCLE OF CODEPENDENT RELATIONSHIPS

Codependent relationships often trap individuals in a repeating loop where their sense of self becomes tied to the needs and emotions of others, creating a fragile balance that's difficult to break. This cycle feeds on patterns of people-pleasing, fear of abandonment, and emotional fusion, where boundaries blur and one's identity is overshadowed by the desire to maintain connection at any cost. The painful reality is that losing yourself in this dynamic can cost your emotional health and vitality, leaving you exhausted and overwhelmed. Yet, recognizing these repeating patterns is the first step toward reclaiming your autonomy and building connections that nurture both partners equally. Embracing the challenge to disrupt this cycle opens the door to healthier, more resilient relationships rooted in interdependence rather than unhealthy reliance or control.

People-Pleasing, Fear, and Emotional Fusion Dynamics

One of the core patterns that keeps codependent relationships spinning in circles is people-pleasing. It's not just about wanting to be liked or accepted—it often runs much deeper, tied to an ingrained fear of abandonment or rejection. When people-pleasing takes hold, individuals start prioritizing others' needs and emotions so heavily that they lose sight of their own boundaries and desires. Over time, this can create a dangerous feedback loop where personal identity blurs into the other person's expectations, leading to what psychologists often refer to as emotional fusion.

People who struggle with codependency often grow up learning that love and approval aren't unconditional. They might have felt that affection was only earned by meeting certain standards, fulfilling specific roles, or consistently putting others first. As adults, this turns into an almost automatic impulse to make others comfortable, happy, or safe—sometimes at the expense of their own emotional health. This impulse isn't just about kindness; it's driven by a profound fear that if they don't keep up, they'll be abandoned or unloved. That fear naturally fuels excessive people-pleasing.

Emotional fusion is a key player in this dynamic. When two people are emotionally fused, their feelings and identities merge so completely that they struggle to tell where one person ends and the other begins. It might feel like being deeply connected, but in codependent relationships, this fusion often comes with a loss of emotional autonomy. Instead of two individuals supporting each other's growth, there's a smothering of individuality. The constant need to be attuned to the partner's state, combined with a reliance on their approval, makes it hard to maintain a stable sense of self.

Fear sits at the root of this fusion and the people-pleasing that feeds it. This fear isn't always loud or apparent; sometimes it's a low-level anxiety or a persistent inner voice warning that something will go wrong if needs aren't met or if emotions aren't carefully managed. It can be fear of abandonment, fear of conflict, or fear of being seen as inadequate. Regardless, it causes people to suppress authentic feelings and play roles rather than bringing their whole selves to the relationship. That suppression can build resentment and disconnect, even while the fear drives them to keep trying harder to please.

Another aspect of this cycle is how fear amplifies the need for control in subtle ways. When someone is constantly trying to keep peace and avoid triggering discomfort in their partner, they're, in effect, trying to control the emotional atmosphere. This often leads to walking on eggshells or second-guessing every word and action to avoid displeasing the other. Sadly, this constant tension undercuts genuine connection. Instead of feeling free and safe, both partners may feel constrained—one trying to maintain control to feel secure, the other reacting to that control with their own fears and defenses.

People-pleasing in this context doesn't mean simply being kind or generous. It's a survival mechanism that's often learned early on and reinforced repeatedly. The difference shows up in motivation—people-pleasing in codependency often comes without awareness, driven by compulsion rather than choice. It's the difference between wanting to support your partner because you care and feeling like you have no choice but to do so to avoid losing them. This lack of choice can leave you feeling trapped and depleted over time.

Emotional fusion breaks down the boundaries required for healthy interdependence. When boundaries are missing or weak, relationships become a tug-of-war for emotional survival instead of partnerships built on mutual respect. Without boundaries, feelings, thoughts, and responsibilities can get jumbled together. This makes it nearly impossible to differentiate which emotions belong to whom, leading to confusion and frustration.

In many codependent relationships, this fusion creates a dynamic where the emotional experience of one partner dictates the emotional and behavioral responses of the other. If one partner feels anxious or upset, the other might instantly feel responsible for calming or fixing those feelings. It becomes exhausting, as no one gets a chance to process their own emotions independently. Both partners end up walking a delicate line, emotionally enmeshed yet often feeling misunderstood or unseen on a deeper level.

Fear also plays a significant role in discouraging healthy confrontation, which is essential for breaking the cycle. Fear of upsetting the balance or triggering a partner's dissatisfaction often leads to avoidance of essential conversations. Instead of addressing concerns openly, communication stays surface-level or laden with passive aggression. This further fuels mistrust and emotional disconnection, making it harder for the relationship to grow authentically.

One of the most challenging things about these dynamics is how normal they can feel when you're living them. The intense emotional interdependence and constant people-pleasing may feel like love or care because they're so interwoven with how you relate to others. That makes it tough to see these patterns as unhealthy, especially if they've been part of your relationship blueprint for years. Recognizing the difference requires learning to listen to your own needs and feelings without judgment—a radical shift for many people caught in codependency.

Despite how difficult this can be, moving away from emotional fusion and compulsive people-pleasing is the foundation for healthier, more interdependent relationships. It means learning to say no without fear, expressing your own needs and emotions honestly, and understanding that your value isn't dependent on constant approval. Fear doesn't disappear overnight, but with patience and practice, it becomes something you can acknowledge without letting it control your behavior.

Building emotional boundaries is essential here. Boundaries don't mean shutting others out; they mean protecting your emotional clarity and strength, so you can engage from a place of genuine choice rather than compulsion. It's about creating space to know who you are and what you want apart from anyone else's expectations or pressures. This space allows for relationships where both people feel respected as whole individuals rather than extensions of each other's emotional needs.

In practice, detaching from emotional fusion doesn't mean cutting off empathy or care. Instead, it's learning to tune into your partner's feelings without absorbing them or feeling responsible for solving every emotional wave. It's a balance that can feel unfamiliar at first but ultimately creates more room for authentic intimacy. When you stand firm in your own emotional center, you invite your partner to do the same, opening the door for a more genuine connection.

Facing the fears that fuel people-pleasing is a courageous step. It requires acknowledging the vulnerability beneath the behavior and taking risks—like speaking your truth or setting limits—even when it feels uncomfortable. It's important to remember that these fears are often echoes of past wounds, not reflections of your present reality. With time and support, you can learn to manage fear instead of being ruled by it.

Ultimately, breaking free from the cycle of people-pleasing, fear, and emotional fusion reshapes how you relate—not just to others but to yourself. It's about reclaiming your emotional autonomy and stepping into relationships that honor both connection and individuality. This balance is what true interdependence looks like: partnerships where love and respect flow both ways, rooted in freedom rather than fear.

The High Cost of Losing Yourself in Relationships

One of the most painful truths of codependent relationships is how much you risk losing your own identity in the process of trying to hold things together. When the focus shifts almost entirely to the needs, emotions, and desires of your partner—often at the expense of your own—you begin to fade into the background of your own life. It doesn't happen overnight, but slowly and almost imperceptibly, the person you once knew can become a shadow of themselves. The cost isn't just emotional exhaustion; it's a profound disconnect from who you truly are.

At the heart of codependency lies a tendency to derive your sense of worth through the eyes and approval of the other person. It feels safer to mold and shape yourself into what you think they want rather than risk rejection or conflict by asserting your real feelings or needs. While this might look like self-sacrifice or devotion on the surface, it's really a kind of self-erasure. You're not just prioritizing someone else—you're giving over control of your own happiness and well-being. Over time, this can drain your emotional reserves and create a deep feeling of emptiness that's hard to explain.

Relationships are about connection, yes, but healthy relationships are built on two whole individuals who come together, not two halves trying desperately to make a whole. When codependency dominates, you lose sight of this important balance. Instead of two separate, autonomous people linking arms, you become entangled in a messy web where boundaries blur, and emotional fusion takes hold. You might find yourself increasingly anxious about your partner's feelings or behaviors, constantly adjusting your own to keep the peace or avoid disappointment.

That constant caretaking role wears you down. It's exhausting to always be the one managing emotions, smoothing out conflict, or anticipating needs without asking for much in return. The impact goes beyond mental and emotional strain; it touches every aspect of your life, including your ability to set goals, pursue passions, or maintain other meaningful relationships. You might notice you've stopped nurturing other friendships or stepping into opportunities that excite you because your focus is perpetually fixed on "making things work" with your partner.

The cost of losing yourself doesn't just show up in the moment—it also casts a long shadow over your sense of self-esteem and confidence. When you continually put others first at the expense of your own voice, you begin to doubt your judgment and question your value outside of the relationship context. It leaves you vulnerable to feeling "less than" or unworthy if the relationship doesn't go well, even though the underlying issue isn't about you being flawed but about the unhealthy dynamics you've been caught in.

Eventually, this lack of self-awareness and diminished autonomy can create a cycle where you feel trapped and powerless. You may start to believe that without this relationship, or this person's approval, you don't know who you are or how to function. This dependency reinforces itself, making the idea of stepping back terrifying. Losing yourself becomes a double-edged sword—you give up your freedom to keep a semblance of connection, only to feel increasingly disconnected on the inside.

It's important to recognize that losing yourself in relationships doesn't happen because you lack strength or character. In fact, it often stems from a deep desire to be loved, accepted, and safe. Many people who experience this are highly empathetic, kind, and willing to give endlessly, but they lack the tools or awareness needed to protect their own boundaries. This sacrifice may even be invisible to others because you've mastered the art of keeping everything smooth and avoiding confrontation.

The emotional toll can also manifest physically. Stress from suppressing your needs, constant worry, and self-denial often contribute to symptoms like fatigue, headaches, and sleep disturbances. Your body is a clear communicator of what your mind and heart may not admit: you're under strain and out of alignment with your true self. Ignoring these signals allows the cost to mount unnoticed—but it doesn't mean the price isn't being paid.

On a deeper level, losing touch with yourself restricts your ability to grow. Personal growth requires self-awareness, reflection, and sometimes the courage to make difficult choices. If you're caught in emotional fusion or people-pleasing cycles, you might shy away from confronting the hard truths because it risks upsetting the fragile balance you've tried to maintain. This can leave you stuck in patterns, repeating the same relationship dynamics that never really meet your needs.

Consider the frustration and sadness that comes from suppressing your authentic desires or opinions just to keep someone else happy. Over time, this leads to resentment—a heavy burden to carry silently. That unresolved resentment eventually seeps into the relationship itself, subtly eroding trust, intimacy, and mutual respect. When you don't honor your own voice, you signal that your feelings don't matter. This invites your partner to unconsciously take more and more, widening the imbalance further.

The cost of losing yourself is also deeply connected to your future happiness. If you surrender your identity today, you risk building a life together on unstable, unsustainable ground. Without the foundation of both partners feeling valued and true to themselves, the relationship's health will inevitably suffer. This isn't about blaming your partner or suggesting you're at fault—it's about recognizing how codependent patterns quietly carve away at personal dignity and emotional well-being.

Regaining yourself within relationship dynamics often means acknowledging the full weight of this cost. It's not just "making time for yourself" but a profound commitment to rediscovering who you are beyond the roles you've played. That includes reclaiming your thoughts, desires, boundaries, and dreams. It might feel risky or uncomfortable at first because it challenges the status quo that has kept the relationship superficially intact.

But the payoff is worth it. When you reclaim your identity, you build a stronger, more resilient foundation, not only for yourself but for the relationship as well. By bringing your whole, authentic self forward, you enable genuine connection to happen—where both partners can thrive instead of just survive. Freedom and love don't have to be opposing forces; they're both possible when you nourish your unique identity alongside your connection to others.

Escaping the costly trap of losing yourself calls for courage, patience, and a shift in how you view relationships. It's about moving from dependence to healthy interdependence—where both people support one another's growth without giving up who they are. That balance nurtures respect, trust, and deep emotional fulfillment. And while this journey isn't easy, it's the path to living fully, freely, and with heart intact.

CHAPTER 4

RED FLAGS IN TOXIC PARTNERSHIPS

Recognizing the warning signs in toxic relationships can be tricky because they often creep in gradually, making it easy to dismiss or rationalize unhealthy dynamics. It's important to trust your instincts when you notice patterns like frequent criticism, emotional withdrawal, or the subtle undermining of your confidence—these aren't just annoyances but signals that your well-being is at risk. Toxic partnerships often mask control and manipulation under the guise of care or concern, leaving you feeling confused and drained. Understanding these red flags early on is a crucial step toward reclaiming your emotional freedom, allowing you to break free from cycles that keep you stuck and instead move toward relationships where both partners grow with respect and mutual support.

Gaslighting, Guilt-Tripping, and Emotional Manipulation Indicators

Recognizing the signs of gaslighting, guilt-tripping, and emotional manipulation is crucial for anyone trying to break free from toxic relationship patterns. These behaviors often sneak into partnerships disguised as concern, love, or just "having a tough time." Yet, beneath the surface, they chip away at your sense of reality, self-worth, and emotional autonomy. Awareness is the first step toward reclaiming your power and reshaping how you relate to others.

Gaslighting is a particularly insidious form of emotional abuse that distorts your perception of truth. It often starts subtly. You might find yourself doubting small things—what you said, what you remember, or how you feel. Your partner might say, "You're overreacting," "That never happened," or "You're too sensitive." Over time, those little comments stack up, making you question your own judgment and sanity. It's important to understand that gaslighting isn't just about lying; it's about systematically undermining your confidence in your reality.

Emotional manipulation, while broader in scope, shares some overlap with gaslighting. Manipulation aims to shape your behavior or decisions to serve someone else's needs, often at your expense. This might show up in the form of strategic appeals to your fears, insecurities, or kindness. A manipulative partner might use phrases like "If you really loved me, you would…" or "I'm the only one who cares about you." These statements create pressure and guilt that aren't grounded in mutual respect, but rather in control.

Guilt-tripping is one of the most common tools in the manipulative toolbox. It plays on your natural desire to be a good partner and to avoid conflict. This tactic often makes you feel responsible for your partner's emotional states or problems, even when it's unfair. For example, if you decline an invitation or express a need, the response may be disappointment or anger framed as your fault. Statements like "I guess I'm just not important to you" or "You don't care about me at all" aim to make you feel shame and second-guess your boundaries.

One indicator of these behaviors is a persistent pattern rather than isolated incidents. Toxic partners rarely gaslight or guilt-trip just once or twice; these tactics become woven into how they communicate and solve conflict. If you notice repeated cycles where your feelings are dismissed, your memories questioned, or you feel pressured to meet unreasonable emotional demands, that's a serious red flag. You deserve to live without walking on eggshells or feeling mentally drained by constant questioning of your reality.

Another subtle sign lies in how your emotional responses are treated. In healthy relationships, your feelings are acknowledged and validated, even when people disagree. But when gaslighting or manipulation is involved, your emotions might be minimized or weaponized against you. You could hear, "Why are you making such a big deal out of nothing?" or

"You're just trying to start a fight." This invalidation creates an internal conflict, pushing you to suppress what you genuinely feel just to keep the peace.

Notice how decisions are made in the relationship. If your partner consistently pressures you to conform to their wishes by invoking guilt or questioning your motivations, that's manipulation. For instance, they might say, "After everything I've done for you, this is how you repay me?" or "If you follow through with this, I'll be devastated." These are emotional traps designed to steer you away from asserting your needs. It's a way to maintain control without direct confrontation.

The impact of these dynamics on your self-esteem can be devastating. Over time, you might start internalizing the negative messages, believing that you're the problem or that your needs don't matter. Often, people in these situations can't pinpoint exactly why they feel so stuck or drained—they just know that they're constantly apologizing or walking on eggshells. That emotional exhaustion isn't normal. Recognizing gaslighting, guilt-tripping, and manipulation allows you to see clearly that the problem lies not within you, but in the way you've been treated.

Another important indicator is the use of "love" or "care" as a conditional weapon. Toxic partners sometimes frame their manipulative tactics as acts of love or protection, which confuses the person being targeted. You might hear, "I'm only this way because I love you so much," or "I'm trying to protect you from getting hurt." While it's natural for people to want to protect those they care about, these statements cross a line when they become tools for controlling behavior. True love supports autonomy rather than limits it.

Isolation often goes hand in hand with these toxic patterns. If a partner is gaslighting or manipulating you, they may try to alienate you from friends, family, or support systems. This cuts off your sources of outside perspective and emotional help, making the manipulation more effective. You may notice subtle discouragement about spending time with others, or outright criticism aimed at your support people, alongside the emotional tactics.

In the thick of emotional manipulation, it's easy to overlook boundary violations. Manipulative partners often test and push limits under the guise of closeness or intimacy. They may demand excessive time, insist on controlling your choices, or criticize you when you assert yourself. Each violation chips away at your independence, making it harder to maintain a sense of self. Learning to recognize these patterns is key to rebuilding and maintaining your emotional autonomy.

Because toxic partners often excel at disguise, trust your intuition when something feels "off." If you consistently feel confused, guilty without reason, or doubting your own perceptions, pause and assess the relationship dynamics. Ask yourself whether your experiences align with what is being portrayed or if there's a disconnect. This kind of reflection, though sometimes uncomfortable, is critical for breaking free from manipulation.

It can help to write down specific interactions that leave you feeling unsettled. Journaling your thoughts and feelings provides concrete evidence to counter the twisting of facts or emotional gaslighting. It's hard to question your own reality when you have documented experiences to look back on. This practice also strengthens self-awareness, helping you notice recurring tactics rather than dismissing them as "just misunderstandings."

Being on high alert for these signs doesn't mean becoming hypervigilant or paranoid. Instead, it's about developing a healthy skepticism toward harmful patterns so you can protect your emotional well-being. Cultivating this awareness opens the door to making conscious choices about who you allow in your life and how you engage with them. It also lays the foundation for setting and enforcing boundaries that honor your needs.

Most importantly, recognizing these indicators isn't about blaming yourself for what's happened. It's about reclaiming your right to feel safe, respected, and heard. Emotional manipulation thrives in the shadows of confusion and self-doubt. Bringing these behaviors into the light breaks their power and enables healing. As you work toward balanced and interdependent relationships, knowing these red flags will keep you grounded and empowered.

In summary, watch for persistent denial of your feelings or memories, constant pressure to meet unfair emotional demands, guilt used as a leash, and any attempts to isolate you from your support systems. Notice if love is ever used as a weapon or if your boundaries are systematically ignored. These are not just signs of a difficult relationship—they are warning signals of emotional harm. Responding to them with clarity and courage is a vital step toward the freedom and connection you deserve.

How to Recognize When You're Being Controlled

Spotting control in a relationship isn't always straightforward. It rarely arrives with a flashing sign or an obvious warning label. Instead, it often starts with small actions and subtle shifts that chip away at your sense of self and freedom. Recognizing when you're being controlled is the first critical step toward reclaiming your autonomy and building healthier bonds. This awareness helps not just in romantic engagements, but also with family, friends, or coworkers who might inadvertently—or intentionally—undermine your independence.

One of the most common ways control manifests is through a steady erosion of your personal choices. If you notice that decisions about your life—big or small—are being questioned, dismissed, or outright vetoed by another person, chances are control is at play. This might look like your partner insisting on how you spend your time, demanding to know your every move, or making you feel guilty for wanting to follow your own path. It's not always loud and confrontational. Sometimes it's a quiet but persistent pressure to conform, comply, or put someone else's desires above your own needs.

Another key indicator is the way communication happens. When conversations frequently leave you feeling confused, doubting your own perceptions, or apologizing for things that shouldn't be your fault, you might be facing manipulation. This is especially true if the person employs tactics like gaslighting, where they deny facts, twist reality, or make you question your memory. Over time, these patterns can subtly adjust your mind's compass. You start to second-guess what you know to be true. That's a dangerous place because it undermines your confidence and primes you for deeper control.

Control can also appear in how your boundaries are treated—or ignored. Boundaries are the invisible lines we draw to preserve our emotional, mental, and physical well-being. If these boundaries are repeatedly crossed, dismissed, or ridiculed, this isn't a sign of caring or concern, but rather a method of control. It might look like pressure to share more than you're comfortable with, getting pushed into situations against your will, or being belittled for saying no. Over time, ignoring your boundaries sends a message that your feelings and limits don't matter, which directly weakens your sense of self-respect.

Feeling isolated or cut off from your support system is another red flag. Controllers often work to limit your connections with friends, family, or anyone who might offer a fresh perspective or support. If you find that your relationships with others are being monitored, restricted, or undermined, that's a sign someone may be trying to monopolize your emotional world. This isolation makes you more dependent on the controlling individual, which is exactly what they want. Healthy relationships encourage you to nurture a broad, diverse network—not to shackle you to just one person's influence.

Watch for patterns of intimidation, whether overt or subtle. Control doesn't always come in the form of loud threats or anger. It may hide in passive-aggressive comments, constant criticism, silent treatments, or the withholding of affection as punishment. These behaviors create an environment where you're always trying to "get it right" or avoid triggering negative reactions. Living in that state of heightened alertness drains your emotional energy and wears down your will to assert yourself. You start prioritizing peace over your own needs, which ultimately reinforces the controlling dynamic.

One tricky aspect of control is that it's often disguised as "love" or "care." Someone might say they're controlling because they want what's best for you or because they fear losing you. While concern is a natural part of close relationships, it crosses into control when it consistently overrides your own feelings, opinions, and choices. It can sound like, "I'm only asking because I love you" or "If you really cared, you'd do this for me." Don't let these statements blur the line between genuine care and manipulation. True love respects autonomy, even when it means stepping back.

It's essential to examine how much you feel free to express yourself in the relationship. Are you able to share your thoughts, dreams, fears, and frustrations without fear of reprisal? Or do you tiptoe around certain topics to avoid conflict or disappointment? If you find yourself censoring your voice or suppressing parts of who you are, that's a warning signal. Control thrives on silence and invisibility. Being able to speak honestly and be heard with respect is a hallmark of healthy connection, not control.

Take note of how decisions get made around you. Do you participate fully, or do you often feel like decisions are imposed on you without your input? Control often shows up through unilateral decision-making, where one person holds all the power and others are expected to follow suit. If you're living with this imbalance, it'll gradually strip away your agency and leave you feeling powerless. Recognizing this early can motivate you to reclaim your voice and negotiate a more equal dynamic.

Often, people who are being controlled experience a mix of emotions that conflict with each other. You might feel love and care, but also fear, confusion, or frustration. You face moments of doubt about whether what you're experiencing is really unhealthy. This internal tug-of-war is normal and to be expected. Control doesn't always present in black and white, which makes it all the more important to trust your instincts and feelings. If something doesn't feel right, it probably isn't.

Learning to recognize subtle signs can be challenging, especially if control has woven itself deeply into the fabric of a relationship over time. Sometimes what feels like "normal" might actually be a pattern you've adapted to without realizing the toll it's taking on your well-being. That's why self-reflection and support from trusted others are crucial. Sharing what you're experiencing with someone outside of the relationship can provide clarity and help you see things from a different angle.

Ultimately, recognizing control involves paying close attention to your emotional and mental freedom. Are you able to pursue your goals without unnecessary restriction? Do you have space to be your authentic self without judgment or pressure? Can you rely on your own judgment, or are you constantly bending to someone else's will? Answering these questions honestly will illuminate whether control is present and help you take steps towards healthier interdependence.

Remember, no one deserves to be controlled or condensed into a shadow of their own potential. Relationships grounded in respect and care empower each person to grow independently while staying connected. Recognizing control marks the beginning of a journey back to that balance.

CHAPTER 5

The First Step—Building Self-Awareness

Taking that initial step toward healthier, more balanced relationships begins with building genuine self-awareness—knowing your feelings, recognizing your patterns, and understanding what drives your reactions without judgment. It's not about blaming yourself for past mistakes or unhealthy habits but about shining a light on behaviors that no longer serve you, so you can start reclaiming your emotional freedom. Developing self-awareness helps you catch those automatic responses and unconscious codependent tendencies early, empowering you to make different choices moving forward. This journey requires patience and compassion, as true change starts with simply noticing where you stand today, preparing you to set boundaries, strengthen self-worth, and ultimately cultivate deeper, more interdependent connections where both you and those you love can truly thrive.

Journaling Prompts and Reflection Tools for Self-Discovery

Stepping into self-awareness is like opening a door to a room you've never fully explored before. It's thrilling but can also feel overwhelming at times. Journaling becomes your flashlight in this new space, helping illuminate patterns, feelings, and thoughts that typically stay hidden beneath the surface. When you're working to break free from codependent cycles and build healthier, interdependent relationships, journaling isn't just about writing—it's an act of self-discovery, a way to know yourself on a deeper, more compassionate level.

Some people think journaling means sitting down and writing pages of intricate detail every day. That's not true. Journaling can be simple, flexible, and tailored to what you need most. The goal isn't perfection or even consistency at first—it's honesty. As you begin, try loosening the grip on expectations and instead focus on being open with yourself. Let your feelings and thoughts spill onto the page without judgment. This approach transforms journaling into a powerful reflection tool rather than just a task to complete.

To help you get started, here are some practical journaling prompts designed specifically for self-discovery within the context of recognizing and unlearning codependent behaviors.

INTERDEPENDENCE RELATIONSHIPS

These prompts encourage you to connect with core values, reflect on emotions, and identify patterns that might have escaped your notice before.

1. **What are three patterns I notice repeating in my relationships?** Consider both positive and negative cycles. Write about moments when you felt connected and moments when you lost your sense of self. This reflection digs at the heart of how codependency often manifests and helps you tune into triggers and behaviors.

2. **When do I most often feel the urge to people-please or sacrifice my needs?** Explore what drives you in those moments. Is it fear of rejection, desire for approval, or a need for control? Getting curious about your motivation helps build awareness without adding guilt.

3. **What feelings am I uncomfortable expressing, and why?** This prompt encourages you to name emotions and also to understand the barriers keeping you from sharing them. Identifying these feelings is the first step toward expressing your true self openly and assertively.

4. **How do I react when someone sets a boundary with me?** Notice your immediate thoughts and feelings. Are you defensive, anxious, or dismissive? Exploring your reactions offers

insight into how boundaries challenge your current relationship dynamics and your own self-view.

5. **What messages about love and worth did I learn in childhood?** Reflect on the stories you were told or the behaviors you observed about relationships and self-value. These early lessons shape how you approach intimacy today, often unconsciously.

6. **When was the last time I put my needs first, and what happened?** Writing about this moment helps you observe your comfort level with self-prioritization. Pay attention to any feelings of guilt or worry, and consider how stepping into self-care can feel revolutionary but necessary.

7. **What does a healthy relationship look like to me?** Describe qualities, behaviors, and dynamics that feel safe and balanced. This exercise aids in clarifying your relationship goals and builds a vision that moves beyond codependency.

8. **Who am I outside of my relationships?** This prompt is about rediscovering your individuality. Write about your passions, dreams, strengths, and characteristics that define you on your own terms, independent of others' opinions or needs.

9. **How do I handle feelings of loneliness or boredom when I'm alone?** Explore your coping mechanisms without shame or judgment.

Understanding your emotional self-sufficiency is key to building interdependence, which allows space for both connection and autonomy.

10. **What support do I need right now to foster my growth?** Identify people, practices, or boundaries that could nurture your healing journey. Writing this down makes your needs clearer and encourages proactive steps toward fulfilling them.

By regularly engaging with prompts like these, you're not only learning about your behaviors and emotions but also practicing the very skill of self-reflection that underpins healthy relationships. This kind of journaling helps you witness your experiences without shame or criticism. When you see your patterns clearly, you gain power: power to choose differently, to interrupt old cycles, and to treat yourself with kindness rather than judgment.

It's also useful to include tools beyond written prompts to deepen your insight. For instance, try introducing free-form writing sessions where you jot down whatever comes to mind without editing. This stream-of-consciousness method can surface buried feelings and ideas you weren't consciously aware of. Sometimes just setting a timer for 5-10 minutes and writing nonstop can reveal unexpected truths.

Another reflection tool is tracking emotional responses throughout your day or week. Create a simple log where you note instances that stir strong emotions, like frustration, sadness, or anxiety. Next to each, write down what triggered the feeling, how you reacted, and how your body felt in that moment. This turns journaling into an ongoing process that sharpens your emotional awareness over time. When you recognize emotional patterns linked to codependency—such as feeling responsible for someone else's mood—you can start creating healthier responses.

Because codependency often involves shame and self-criticism, incorporating gratitude and self-compassion into your journaling is vital. At least once a week, write about things you appreciate about yourself or moments you handled a situation with courage—even if imperfectly. Shifting your mindset to acknowledge growth rather than failure is a foundational part of moving toward balanced interdependence.

Some find it helpful to develop a personal mantra or affirmation through journaling. For example, you might write: "I am allowed to set boundaries that protect my well-being" or "My worth is not tied to others' approval." Repeating these affirmations regularly, and writing them down, reinforces new beliefs that counter old codependent conditioning. Over time, this practice nurtures a resilient, confident core within you.

It's normal for journaling to feel challenging or uncomfortable at first. Facing parts of yourself that have been hidden or denied takes courage. If emotions become intense, pause and remind yourself this is a safe space to explore. You're not alone, and seeking outside support from a therapist or support group can be a powerful complement to your journaling work. The goal is progress, not perfection.

In summary, journaling prompts and reflection tools function as a mirror for the soul during your journey to build self-awareness. They invite you to look honestly at your thoughts, feelings, and behaviors, especially those related to relationship patterns. With patience and consistent practice, these exercises expand your understanding of who you are beyond codependency and pave the way toward healthier, more fulfilling connections rooted in mutual respect and autonomy.

Remember, self-discovery is dynamic—not a one-time achievement but an ongoing process. As you grow, your reflections and the way you journal will evolve too. Allow yourself the grace to revisit prompts, update your insights, and celebrate the small wins. Each step taken with intention builds a stronger foundation for the interdependent relationships you deserve.

Noticing Codependent Patterns Without Shame

Recognizing codependent behaviors in yourself can feel overwhelming at first. It's common to stumble upon these patterns and immediately judge yourself harshly. But shame isn't helpful here—it only keeps you stuck in the cycle, blinding you from seeing the truth with clarity and compassion. The first crucial step in building self-awareness is observing these behaviors without shame or self-condemnation. This means treating your discovery like you would a friend's: with kindness, curiosity, and a desire to understand rather than criticize.

Codependency often shows up subtly, woven into the fabric of your daily interactions rather than flashing like a neon sign. You might notice an impulse to prioritize others' needs even when it drains you, or a quiet fear that saying no will lead to rejection or conflict. Maybe there's a habit of constantly seeking reassurance or feeling responsible for others' emotions. These aren't signs of weakness or failure—they're coping mechanisms developed over time. When you spot these patterns, pause and take a deep breath. Acknowledge what you're noticing without immediately leaping to "I'm broken" or "I'm too much." Instead, say something like, "This is a part of me that's trying to survive."

It's also important to remember that codependence isn't about blaming yourself or your partner. These patterns often trace back to early life experiences, where emotional survival meant learning to tune in closely to others' moods or hide your own true feelings. Recognizing those roots helps soften the impulse to shame yourself. When you notice these behaviors creeping in, try to write them down or mentally note them without judgment. This tracking is more than just an exercise; it's creating space between you and your automatic reactions. That space is the foundation for real choice and change.

One reason shame tends to take hold is that codependent patterns are frequently misunderstood, even by those experiencing them. Society often frames "people-pleasing" or "being overly caring" as virtues, so when those tendencies result in personal pain or loss of self, it feels confusing and contradictory. You might wonder, "If I'm so caring, why am I hurting?" This disconnect fuels guilt and shame. But what you're really facing is an imbalance, where giving and pleasing have tipped too far toward self-sacrifice. By seeing your codependent traits clearly and kindly, you can begin to reclaim balance in the way you relate to others.

Another key aspect is recognizing that noticing these patterns isn't a one-time event. Self-awareness is a continual process, a practice that deepens over time. Sometimes you'll be mindful of your emotional fusion with a partner or your urge to fix someone else's problems right away, and other times it might sneak past your radar. That's okay. Progress isn't about perfection—it's about becoming more conscious of the dynamics shaping your life. Keeping a journal or using reflection prompts can be incredibly helpful in cultivating this ongoing awareness. Writing about your interactions, your feelings before and after conversations, and your physical sensations can shed light on unconscious habits.

When you do catch yourself slipping into codependent behaviors, it's powerful to pause and ask gentle questions: What am I feeling right now? What am I needing? Am I doing this out of fear or love? These questions open doors to your internal world, helping you differentiate between healthy care and unhealthy compulsion. Over time, this kind of inquiry weakens the grip of shame because it shifts your focus from "What's wrong with me?" to "What do I need to thrive?"

It's natural to feel vulnerable when facing the truth about your relationship patterns, especially if those patterns have caused pain or confusion for years. Vulnerability can feel like exposure, and that's scary. But vulnerability, in this context, is also a form of courage and self-respect. It means you're willing to look beneath the surface and sift through uncomfortable emotions rather than pushing them down or ignoring them. This willingness is the heart of self-awareness and the gateway to healing.

Often, people try to shield themselves from shame by avoiding self-reflection altogether or by deflecting blame onto others. While it's understandable to protect yourself, this avoidance prolongs the cycle of codependence. Real transformation starts with acceptance—embracing the whole picture of your emotional landscape, even the messy parts. When you see your codependent tendencies clearly without judgment, you gain the power to choose differently.

One more thing to keep in mind: codependent patterns don't define your worth. No matter how deeply ingrained these behaviors feel, they are habits, not identity traits. They are patterns learned and reinforced but absolutely changeable. You are not your codependency. You are a whole person with the ability to grow beyond these limiting dynamics. Relinquishing shame opens up space for self-compassion, the essential ingredient in rebuilding your self-worth and developing healthier, more balanced relationships.

As you practice noticing your codependent patterns without shame, you may also find it helpful to connect with others who understand the journey. Sometimes, sharing your experiences with supportive friends, mentors, or support groups can bring relief by normalizing what you're going through.

Knowing you're not alone often lessens shame and cultivates a sense of belonging and hope.

Remember, every step toward awareness—no matter how small—is a victory. Each moment you witness a codependent impulse with kindness instead of criticism, you're rewiring your brain to respond differently next time. This shift creates the foundation for healthier connection on your path toward interdependence where mutual respect, personal boundaries, and emotional resilience flourish.

Your journey toward freedom from codependency begins right here—with the brave act of noticing patterns without shame.

CHAPTER 6

Setting Boundaries Without Guilt

Learning to set boundaries is one of the most powerful steps toward reclaiming your emotional freedom and building healthier connections, yet it often comes wrapped in guilt and second-guessing. This guilt usually stems from old patterns where your needs were minimized or dismissed, making you feel selfish when you assert yourself. But boundaries aren't about shutting others out; they're about honoring your worth and creating space for mutual respect, trust, and balance. When you approach boundaries as acts of self-love rather than confrontation, you open the door to relationships where both people can grow without losing themselves. It's not always easy, especially at first, but understanding that saying "no" or "this isn't okay" protects your wellbeing is what breaks the cycle of codependency and invites deeper, more resilient interdependence.

Why Boundaries Are Acts of Love and Self-Respect

Setting boundaries often feels like drawing lines that keep others away. But the truth is far more empowering. Boundaries are not walls but invitations to healthier interactions—they're how you define what you're willing to accept emotionally, mentally, and physically. When you establish a boundary, you're not shutting someone out; you're showing them that you value yourself enough to say, "This is what I need to thrive." It's a profound act of love, not just for yourself but for those around you. It creates space where authentic connections can flourish without the shadow of resentment or burnout.

Many people mistake boundaries for selfishness or rejection because that's the language some unhealthy relationships speak. But in reality, boundaries are the opposite of self-neglect. They say, "I matter, my feelings matter, and my needs deserve respect." If you've spent years in cycles of codependency, it might feel unnatural or even scary to say no or to ask for what you need. That's precisely why setting boundaries is an act of courage and deep self-respect. You're shifting from a mindset of survival to one of thriving, where your well-being is a non-negotiable priority.

What makes boundaries an act of love is how they affect your relationships over time. When you communicate your limits clearly and kindly, you stop the buildup of unspoken frustration and confusion. Without boundaries, resentment quietly grows beneath the surface—resentment that sours your feelings toward the people you care about most. Boundaries foster honesty, trust, and mutual respect. They give others a roadmap for how to treat you well, which strengthens bonds rather than weakening them. So, setting boundaries isn't pushing people away; it's inviting them to show up in ways that honor both of you.

From a self-respect perspective, boundaries are non-negotiables about who you are and what you stand for. They reflect your values and your commitment to yourself. This is especially crucial for those emerging from codependent patterns, where your sense of self was often defined by others' needs or approval. Reclaiming your boundaries helps rebuild your identity piece by piece because it forces you to become clear about what's acceptable and what isn't. Over time, it rewires your relationship with yourself—you begin to trust your own voice and instincts more.

You might wonder why you feel guilty when you set boundaries. This guilt is a common leftover from coping strategies developed in childhood or dysfunctional relationships, where your needs were minimized or dismissed. It's a learned response—one that needs rewriting. Recognizing that boundaries are actually nurturing acts can help reframe that guilt. When you remind yourself that boundaries protect your emotional energy and prevent burnout, it becomes easier to hold them without shame. The self-love behind a boundary dismantles the old programming of codependency that tells you to stay small or invisible for the sake of others.

It's also essential to understand that boundaries help you preserve your capacity for generous, empathic love. When you say yes to everything to avoid conflict or gain approval, you end up depleted and disconnected. You become less available emotionally to others because you've given too much without replenishing yourself. Boundaries act like a fence around your emotional garden—it keeps the weeds of overcommitment and resentment from choking what you want to grow in your relationships. By honoring your limits, you create more room for genuine care, presence, and deeper connection.

Many people worry that setting boundaries will hurt others or make them feel rejected. But honest, consistent boundaries create safer, more predictable relationships. When someone knows what you can and can't tolerate, it reduces uncertainty and power struggles. You stop guessing games and emotional manipulations because you're clear about where you stand. That clarity is actually a gift to everyone involved. It encourages personal responsibility because it doesn't blame or demand—it simply states what's healthy for you.

Think about a healthy boundary as a form of interpersonal respect you both give and receive. You're saying, "I respect myself by protecting my time, emotions, and values, and I respect you enough to be straightforward about them." This honesty invites others to examine their own boundaries, often leading to growth on both sides. It's a ripple effect of self-respect that builds stronger, more balanced connections. In effect, boundaries help everyone evolve beyond codependency's unhealthy patterns into relationships marked by trust, equality, and mutual care.

Even though boundaries are necessary, they require practice and patience to master. Setting boundaries is a skill, not a one-time event. You'll likely face resistance—from others and sometimes even from yourself. That's natural because you're breaking old habits that no longer serve your well-being. But with every boundary you establish, you reinforce your commitment to your own worth. You also teach those around you that your presence matters—not just as a person who gives but as one who deserves respect and authentic connection.

What's truly inspiring about boundaries is how they nurture your sense of freedom. When you honor your limits, you reclaim your power to choose and to shape your life dynamically, rather than feeling trapped. Freedom grows out of respect for yourself and the courage to protect your peace. Boundaries let you lean into relationships without losing yourself because they preserve the vital space where your individuality and connection coexist. You no longer sacrifice your needs for the illusion of harmony; instead, you create harmony that respects your whole self.

In the end, setting boundaries without guilt transforms the way you experience love. It shifts love from being conditional or transactional to something expansive and fulfilling. Boundaries honor your right to self-care and to say no when something doesn't feel right. They allow you to say yes to the things and people who genuinely nourish you. When love grows out of this foundation of respect and boundaries, it becomes deeper, more resilient, and far more rewarding. Every time you set a boundary, you practice walking the delicate balance of interdependence—where independence and connection strengthen each other, rather than compete.

Scripts and Strategies for Saying No Effectively

Learning to say no is fundamental in setting healthy boundaries without guilt. It's not just about rejecting requests; it's about honoring yourself in a way that nurtures interdependent relationships rather than codependent ones. If you've struggled with codependency, saying no might have felt like a betrayal or a source of anxiety. But once you shift the mindset to view no as a form of self-respect and protection, it becomes easier to embrace. The challenge is crafting responses that feel authentic and clear, yet compassionate enough to maintain connection.

One of the biggest obstacles to saying no effectively is fear—fear of disappointing others, fear of conflict, or fear of abandonment. The following scripts aren't rigid formulas but adaptable tools to help you articulate your boundaries with confidence and care. You don't have to explain yourself in detail or apologize excessively. Firm but kind communication works best.

For example, a simple script to decline a request might be: **"I'm not able to take that on right now."** That short sentence honors your limits without over-explaining or feeling defensive. Adding a gentle but honest reason can soften the delivery yet keep the boundary intact. Saying, **"I have other commitments that need my attention"** or **"I need time for myself this week"** expresses your priority without inviting debate or guilt.

At times, you might feel pressure to provide a detailed explanation or justify your no, especially if the person asking is close to you or used to you saying yes. Here, using the "I" statements technique helps. This approach centers your feelings and needs instead of focusing on what the other person wants. Say something like, **"I feel overwhelmed when I say yes to everything, so I have to limit my commitments."** By putting the focus on your reality, you keep the conversation less confrontational and more about your self-care.

Sometimes, people respond with disappointment or insistence. That's when it helps to reiterate your boundary without wavering. A strategy called the "broken record" involves calmly and consistently repeating your no. If someone pushes back, say, **"I understand this is hard, but I can't help with that."** Repeating your boundary calmly sends a clear message that it's not negotiable. Over time, this consistency helps others respect your limits and understand your commitment to them.

It's also valid to delay your answer if you're unsure or feel pressured. Instead of giving an immediate yes or no, you can say, **"I need some time to think about that."** This buys you space to assess your feelings and priorities before committing. Impulse saying yes often leads to resentment or burnout later.

Taking time signals that your boundaries include thoughtful consideration, not just reactive acquiescence.

Kindness doesn't have to be sacrificed when you say no. You can soften your message with appreciation or empathy, which keeps relationship dynamics positive. For instance, saying **"Thanks for thinking of me, but I have to pass on this one"** validates the invitation or request without compromising your boundary. Similarly, **"I know this means a lot to you, and I hope you understand why I can't participate"** shows you care, even while declining. This approach reduces misunderstandings and builds respect.

Avoiding vague or evasive replies is crucial. Saying things like **"Maybe,"** or **"I'm not sure,"** if you really know your answer is no, can create mixed messages and prolong discomfort. Clear communication fosters healthy boundaries, which, in turn, cultivates trust. Saying no clearly—even if it feels uncomfortable at first—lays the groundwork for honest and resilient relationships.

Body language and tone matter just as much as words. Speaking with calmness, steady eye contact, and a neutral to warm tone shows you're confident yet approachable. Avoid sounding apologetic or defensive. If your body language suggests hesitation or guilt, the message becomes weaker and invites pushback. Practicing these scripts aloud can help you develop natural delivery, making each no feel less like a confrontation and more like a self-honoring exchange.

In situations where you want to offer an alternative without saying yes directly, balanced responses help. For example, if declining a request to take on a task at work or household chore, you might say, **"I can't do that this time, but I'm happy to help with something else."** This keeps the relationship collaborative, not rejected, while maintaining your limits.

Another useful strategy is setting boundaries in advance by proactively communicating your limits. If you know certain periods are especially demanding or you need downtime, let people know early: **"I won't be available for extra projects this month."** When people expect the no ahead of time, it reduces awkward moments and increases mutual understanding.

One effective script for difficult conversations revolves around emotional safety. You might express something like, **"I want to support you, but I need to say no this time to protect my own well-being."** This acknowledges relationships are give-and-take, but self-care remains a priority. Naming your emotions helps others see the human side of your boundary, decreasing feelings of rejection.

Learning to say no also involves unlearning old patterns of people-pleasing and codependent behaviors. A part of that is practicing self-compassion when the discomfort arises. Sometimes saying no triggers guilt or fear, especially if you're new to it. Recognize those feelings without judgment, and remind yourself that setting limits is a healthy, necessary act—not a selfish one.

Consider journaling your experiences with saying no—what responses felt right, where friction occurred, and what you'd like to adjust next time. Reflection helps deepen your boundary-setting skills and track progress along your healing journey. Sharing your boundaries clearly becomes easier the more you affirm your right to them.

Lastly, don't hesitate to seek support when boundaries get tested. Trusted friends, support groups, or a therapist can provide encouragement and perspective, especially if you're dealing with persistent pressure from close relationships. You're not alone in learning this skill; it's a process requiring patience and practice. With time, your ability to say no effectively empowers you to build relationships based on honesty, respect, and mutual care.

CHAPTER 7

THE POWER OF SELF-WORTH IN HEALING

Healing from unhealthy relationship patterns starts with reclaiming your sense of self-worth, which acts as the foundation for genuine change. When you begin to see your value from within, rather than relying on outside approval, you break free from the grips of codependency and open the door to emotional freedom. This inner confidence fuels your ability to make choices that honor your true needs and fosters resilience when setbacks occur. Building self-worth isn't about perfection—it's about accepting yourself fully and trusting that you deserve respect, love, and balance. In doing so, you lay the groundwork for healthier connections that support growth without sacrifice or loss of identity.

Rebuilding Confidence from Within

Rebuilding confidence is one of the most crucial steps on the journey to healing from codependency. When unhealthy relationship patterns have chipped away at your self-esteem, it's common to feel fragile, uncertain, or even lost. The good news is that confidence isn't a fixed trait you're born with or without; it can be cultivated and strengthened from the inside out. This process takes time, patience, and a compassionate approach to yourself, but the transformation it brings is nothing short of empowering.

At the heart of rebuilding confidence lies reconnecting with your authentic self—beyond the roles you played or the expectations you felt pressured to meet in your relationships. Too often, codependent dynamics encourage us to put other people's needs, desires, and emotions ahead of our own, creating a feedback loop where our sense of worth becomes tied solely to external validation. Undoing this pattern begins by recognizing that your value exists independently of how others treat you or the approval you might have sought.

It's natural to hesitate when it comes to trusting your capabilities after repeated experiences of feeling overlooked or not heard. Doubts creep in, whispering that you're not enough or that mistakes will only lead to rejection. That's why the process starts with small, deliberate acts to challenge these negative beliefs. Each time you set a boundary, voice a preference, or choose your wellbeing, you give yourself evidence that you deserve respect and care—not just in theory, but in practice.

This rebuilding isn't about suddenly becoming perfect or confident in every situation. It's more about learning to show up for yourself consistently—and forgiving yourself for any moments of weakness along the way. Think of confidence as a muscle: the more you exercise it with realistic challenges, the stronger it gets. When you face fears such as speaking up, saying no, or asserting your feelings, you gather proof that you can handle discomfort and stand firm without losing your identity.

One of the pivotal shifts in this phase involves changing how you talk to yourself. Inner dialogue shapes your emotional world profoundly. Instead of allowing a harsh, critical voice to dominate— the one that magnifies failures or dwells on flaws — work on developing a kinder, more encouraging inner companion. Practicing self-compassion doesn't mean ignoring mistakes, but rather approaching them as opportunities for growth rather than evidence of inadequacy.

Many individuals stuck in codependent cycles have learned to silence their own needs and suppress feelings lest they cause conflict or disappointment. Part of rebuilding confidence is reclaiming permission to feel your emotions fully and express them safely. This means acknowledging moments of sadness, frustration, or anger without judgment or shame. Emotional honesty with yourself is fundamental because it teaches you that your inner landscape is valid and worthy of attention.

Alongside personal reflection, surrounding yourself with people who reinforce your self-worth contributes significantly. Healthy relationships serve as mirrors, reflecting back your qualities and affirming your progress. Finding or creating a support system that encourages your independence rather than feeding dependence allows you space to experiment with new behaviors and receive validation that aligns with your true self. These connections remind you that you're not alone on this path.

Another powerful tool is setting and celebrating achievable goals. These aren't about grand accomplishments but consistent steps that reinforce the idea that you have agency over your life. It could be as simple as asserting yourself in a conversation where you'd previously stayed quiet, or dedicating time each day to a passion or hobby that brings you joy. Every success, no matter how small, adds up to rebuild the foundation of self-trust.

Remember, setbacks are inevitable. The road to rebuilding confidence isn't linear, and moments of doubt or regression might crop up. When they do, it's important to treat these moments with curiosity rather than self-criticism. Ask yourself what these feelings or experiences are teaching you—are there lingering fears to address? Unhealed wounds to nurture? Viewing setbacks as part of the learning curve helps prevent them from becoming reasons to abandon progress.

In the process of strengthening your sense of confidence, it helps to identify and challenge specific internalized messages that undermine your worth. These might include beliefs like "I have to please others to be loved" or "My needs aren't as important." Recognizing these thoughts as distortions rather than truths opens the door to replacing them with healthier perspectives. Over time, you'll notice these old habits of mind losing their grip, allowing a more balanced and affirming self-view to take root.

Rebuilding confidence also involves reconnecting with your strengths and capabilities. It's easy to forget how resilient and resourceful you are when past experiences leave you feeling vulnerable. Taking stock of situations you've navigated successfully—whether overcoming difficult emotions, setting boundaries, or handling challenges—helps remind you of your inherent power. Sometimes listing these strengths or writing about them provides a concrete anchor to counterbalance self-doubt.

Developing a practice of self-validation is key. Unlike seeking approval from others, self-validation means you acknowledge your thoughts, feelings, and efforts as legitimate on their own terms. This doesn't imply arrogance or ignoring feedback, but it means holding space for your experience without immediately doubting it or searching for external confirmation. Over time, this ability creates a secure internal environment where your self-worth can thrive.

It's also vital to cultivate a sense of purpose connected to your values. Confidence grows when your actions align with what truly matters to you, rather than what you think others expect. Clarifying your values leads to choices that feel authentic and fulfilling. This alignment between who you are and how you live cultivates a steady and lasting sense of self-assurance because it's rooted in integrity, not in performance.

Physical self-care plays an important role as well. When you treat your body kindly—whether through rest, nourishment, movement, or relaxation—you send a message of respect and care inward. This bodily attunement enhances your overall sense of wellbeing, which bolsters emotional resilience and confidence. Neglecting your physical needs often goes hand-in-hand with diminished self-worth, so learning to honor yourself holistically supports the whole healing process.

Finally, patience is essential. Confidence rebuilds gradually, not overnight. Each stage of healing brings its own challenges and rewards. By committing to the ongoing practice of self-kindness, truthful self-expression, and boundary-setting, you weave a safety net within yourself that cushions falls and catches you when you feel uncertain. This self-contained source of strength becomes the foundation for creating healthy, balanced relationships that honor both your needs and the needs of others.

Reclaiming your confidence from within is a transformational journey that opens doors to freedom from codependent patterns. It allows you to step into relationships as your whole, empowered self—ready to connect without losing your identity or compromising your worth. This inner rebuilding is the key that unlocks healthier connections, deeper intimacy, and lasting emotional resilience for the future.

Letting Go of Approval Seeking Behaviors

One of the most freeing steps in healing and reclaiming your sense of self-worth is letting go of the need for constant approval from others. When your validation depends on how others see you, it creates a fragile foundation for your self-esteem—one that can crumble with every perceived criticism or rejection. Over time, this approval seeking becomes a heavy weight that keeps you stuck in unhealthy relationship patterns, whether with romantic partners, family, or friends. Releasing this attachment is essential for building the resilient, balanced connections you're striving for.

Approval seeking often starts as a survival mechanism. Maybe you learned early on that love or acceptance was conditional. Perhaps you were rewarded for being "good" or "helpful," but only so long as you stayed within the boundaries others set. This creates a habit of monitoring your behavior and choices through the eyes of others, instead of tuning into your own values, desires, and feelings. Breaking free from this pattern requires a willingness to disrupt long-standing internal scripts and trust yourself more fully, even when it feels uncomfortable.

The craving for others' approval can disguise itself in subtle ways. You might find yourself saying yes to things you don't really want to do, avoiding conflict to keep peace at all costs, or downplaying your achievements because you don't want to seem boastful. These behaviors chip away at your authenticity and create an invisible barrier between who you are and who you feel pressured to be. Over time, this disconnect erodes self-worth, making it easier to fall back into codependent dynamics where your needs get lost.

Letting go doesn't mean becoming indifferent to what others think—it means shifting the source of your worth. Rather than relying on external approval, you learn to validate yourself from within. This internal validation acts as a much sturdier anchor. When your self-worth is grounded in your own sense of who you are—your values, your boundaries, your efforts—you're far less vulnerable to manipulation or emotional highs and lows caused by others' reactions.

This shift takes practice and patience. Start by noticing moments when you automatically seek someone's approval. What are you afraid will happen if you don't get it? Often, it's fear of rejection, abandonment, or feeling unlovable. Naming these fears is an important step to demystify them and see that they often don't reflect reality. It's also beneficial to journal about instances where you made decisions based on others' expectations, then reflect on how that affected your sense of self. Awareness lays the groundwork for change.

Building new habits involves small, intentional acts of self-trust. For example, if you typically ask for feedback before expressing an opinion, try stating your perspective first and observe the outcome. It can feel risky, but each time you practice trusting your voice, you reclaim a bit more of your autonomy. Similarly, setting boundaries is a critical part of this process. When you say no without guilt, you send yourself the message that your needs matter, which undermines the approval-seeking tendency.

Remember, this isn't about perfection or eliminating all sensitivity to others' feelings. Humans are social beings, and connection is vital. The goal is to stop making external approval the primary currency of your self-worth. When you hold that power internally, you can engage in relationships more authentically. You become less reactive to disapproval and more capable of maintaining your integrity, even when disagreements arise.

It's also helpful to challenge the belief that others' opinions define your value. Ask yourself: "Whose voice am I listening to?" If it's a harsh inner critic that echoes messages from past experiences, you can start rewriting that narrative. Replace self-judgment with compassion. Practice affirmations that affirm your worth independent of accomplishments or acceptance. Over time, these mental habits rewire the emotional pathways that used to drive your approval seeking.

Another key point is learning to sit with discomfort. Letting go means facing the possibility that some people might not like or approve of you—and that's okay. Your worth isn't conditional on universal likability. This can feel terrifying at first, but it's also liberating. When you stop trying to control others' perceptions, you free up energy to deepen the relationships where you are genuinely seen and valued.

Peer support or therapy can be invaluable during this journey. Sharing your struggles with approval seeking behaviors in a safe space helps reduce shame and isolation. You'll realize you're not alone; many people wrestle with the same dynamics. Guidance from a skilled professional can assist in identifying underlying wounds and developing personalized strategies for growth.

Letting go also opens up space for interdependence—the balanced connection between autonomy and intimacy that this book emphasizes. When you're not caught in approval cycles, you can show up as your true self, inviting authentic responses rather than conditional acceptance. This fosters respect, trust, and emotional safety for both you and those around you.

Lastly, celebrate your progress along the way. Every time you resist the urge to people-please or base your worth on external validation, acknowledge your courage. Healing is not linear, and setbacks are part of the process. Compassion for yourself fuels resilience, helping you keep moving forward even when the path feels uncertain.

In sum, letting go of approval seeking behaviors is a powerful act of reclaiming your self-worth. It allows you to live with greater freedom, authenticity, and emotional balance. This shift supports healthier, interdependent relationships that honor both your individuality and your connections with others. As you continue to build this foundation, remember that your value has always been intact—you're simply learning to see it clearly and hold it firmly within.

CHAPTER 8

From Reactivity to Response in Relationships

When we shift from reacting impulsively to responding thoughtfully in our relationships, we open the door to healthier, more resilient connections that don't rely on old, automatic patterns. This transition isn't about suppressing emotions or avoiding conflict; it's about recognizing our triggers and choosing how to act instead of letting those triggers dictate our behavior. Developing this kind of emotional regulation takes practice and compassion for ourselves, especially as we learn to pause and breathe before jumping into action. Over time, responding rather than reacting can help break cycles of codependency by encouraging accountability, fostering clear communication, and building trust—not just with others, but within ourselves as well.

Emotional Regulation Techniques for Healthy Interaction

Moving from reactivity to thoughtful response in relationships is a fundamental shift that transforms how we connect with others. Emotional regulation isn't about suppressing feelings or pretending everything is fine; it's about recognizing emotions, managing them constructively, and choosing responses that nurture connection instead of conflict. For those striving to break free from codependency and build strong, interdependent bonds, mastering emotional regulation is an invaluable skill. It creates space for intentional communication and deepens the trust necessary for healthy intimacy.

One crucial step in emotional regulation is developing awareness of your internal emotional landscape. Before any meaningful shift can happen, you have to be able to name what you're feeling in the moment. Is it frustration, sadness, fear, or disappointment? Sometimes multiple emotions arise simultaneously, and identifying them accurately helps prevent the cascade of reactive behaviors often learned in codependent patterns. Journaling or simply pausing to reflect on your feelings—even for a few seconds—can interrupt automatic reactions and lay the groundwork for healthier options.

Breathing techniques play a surprisingly powerful role in calming the nervous system when emotional intensity peaks. Deep, slow breaths engage the parasympathetic nervous system, signaling the body to relax and allowing the mind to regain clarity. Something as simple as a 4-7-8 breath—inhale for 4 seconds, hold for 7, exhale for 8—can mitigate impulsive responses during heated moments. With practice, these techniques become almost instinctual tools to regain composure, making room for more balanced and authentic interaction.

Another effective approach is grounding, which helps anchor you in the present when emotions feel overwhelming or threatening. Grounding exercises range from feeling your feet firmly on the floor to focusing on physical sensations such as the texture of an object or the rhythm of your heartbeat. This sensory focus redirects your attention away from spiraling thoughts or past relational wounds that can hijack emotional responses. Engaging with the here-and-now reduces anxiety and fuels greater self-control in moments when emotions typically run wild.

Alongside awareness and calming strategies, cognitive reframing is a vital technique for emotional regulation in relationships. It encourages shifting your perspective on triggering events or partner behaviors to reduce emotional reactivity. For instance, instead of interpreting a late reply as rejection or abandonment, you might reframe it as your partner being busy or distracted. This subtle mental shift can dampen alarm signals in your brain and open the door to a curious, compassionate approach rather than reactive defensiveness or withdrawal.

Balancing self-compassion with accountability is another cornerstone of effective emotional regulation. It's natural to judge ourselves harshly when feelings feel out of control or responses land poorly. But beating yourself up only fuels shame and keeps old patterns alive. Instead, try treating your emotional upsets with the same kindness you would offer a friend. Self-compassion creates a safer internal environment to explore triggers honestly and make adjustments without paralysis. At the same time, hold yourself responsible for communicating openly and respectfully, recognizing that emotions motivate but don't excuse harmful behaviors.

In the context of developing healthier interactions, emotional regulation also means learning to recognize and honor your boundaries. When triggered, codependency often pushes people toward people-pleasing or retreat instead of expressing real needs. Effective emotional regulation calls for a clear acknowledgement of personal limits and a willingness to articulate those limits calmly. This doesn't just protect your well-being—it invites your partner or loved one into an atmosphere of honesty that supports mutual respect and containment.

It's important to note that emotional regulation is a skill cultivated over time, not a switch you flip overnight. Some days, despite your best efforts, reactions may feel immediate and overpowering. That's part of the journey. Being mindful of such moments without harsh judgment creates opportunities for growth and resilience. With continued practice, even intense emotional waves start to become manageable tides, allowing more conscious choices to guide your interactions.

Another practical technique is the use of "time-outs" during tense exchanges. When conversations escalate and feelings run too high, stepping away for a set period can help prevent damage and promote self-regulation. This pause doesn't mean avoidance; rather, it's a strategic break to check in with your internal state and calm the physiological storm. Returning with fresh energy and a cooler mindset fosters dialogue that is less reactive and more solution-focused.

In addition to individual strategies, emotional regulation benefits greatly from shared efforts between partners or within family dynamics. Developing a mutual language around emotions, such as naming feelings or recognizing signs of distress, creates a team approach to maintaining emotional balance. This cooperative framework strengthens bonds and reduces the isolation that often accompanies reactivity. When both parties feel emotionally safe, they're more likely to respond thoughtfully rather than impulsively.

Practicing mindfulness consistently is another cornerstone of emotional regulation in relationships. Mindfulness teaches you to observe your internal and external experiences without judgment. Over time, this cultivates a greater sense of emotional presence rather than avoidance or fusion. Being fully present with your own feelings and your partner's allows for responses based on curiosity and connection rather than fear or neediness. It nurtures the space where healthy interactions can unfold naturally and with resilience.

Emotional regulation also involves recognizing the impact of stress on your capacity to respond effectively. Chronic stress can lower patience, increase irritability, and disrupt sleep patterns, all of which make healthy interaction harder. Prioritizing self-care routines such as regular exercise, adequate rest, and nourishing nutrition supports your nervous system's ability to self-regulate. When your body and mind are resilient, emotional regulation becomes less daunting and more sustainable.

It's worth mentioning the role of assertiveness within emotional regulation. Learning to express feelings and needs clearly and respectfully, without aggression or passive withdrawal, sustains healthy communication cycles. Assertiveness prevents emotional buildup that leads to explosive reactions or silent resentments. Over time, cultivating this approach enhances both self-confidence and relational trust, setting healthier expectations for interaction patterns.

Finally, remember that emotional regulation doesn't remove vulnerability—it actually invites it in a way that is safe and balanced. When emotions are managed constructively, sharing fears, hopes, and disappointments becomes a pathway to deeper understanding rather than a risk for overwhelming chaos. This balance between openness and regulation is the hallmark of interdependent relationships—where both people show up authentically and choose compassionate responses over reactive defensive maneuvers.

By integrating these emotional regulation techniques, individuals seeking freedom from unhealthy relationship patterns build a foundation for meaningful, lasting connections. Moving beyond reactivity toward intentional response reshapes not only how partners relate to each other, but how each person relates to themselves. With patience, practice, and kindness, emotional regulation becomes a vital tool on the path to relationships grounded in trust, respect, and mutual growth.

Managing Triggers and Maintaining Calm in Connections

Moving from reactivity to a more thoughtful response in relationships starts with understanding what triggers us and learning how to manage those moments before they escalate. Triggers can be subtle or intense—they often pop up unexpectedly and can flood us with emotion before we even realize what's happening. The goal isn't to suppress these feelings but to create space between the trigger and our reaction so that we can engage with our loved ones more mindfully.

Triggers often stem from unresolved wounds or unmet needs, sometimes dating back to childhood experiences or past relationships. When someone unknowingly stumbles upon these tender spots, it's easy to jump into defensive or reactive patterns. Part of healing is recognizing what these triggers are and how they show up in your body and mind. Maybe your heart races, your thoughts spiral, or you feel an urge to withdraw or lash out. These reactions are signals, not commands, and learning to listen to them with curiosity rather than judgment opens a path to calm.

One of the first steps to managing triggers is developing self-awareness in the moment. This means catching yourself as the trigger surfaces—paying attention to your physical sensations, immediate thoughts, and emotional responses. This act of noticing is powerful because it interrupts the automatic nature of reactivity. Instead of being swept away, you're able to ground yourself. Grounding techniques can vary for each person but often include deep breathing, focusing on sensory details around you, or silently naming the emotions you're experiencing. Even a simple pause can create enough of a break to prevent emotional flooding.

Maintaining calm in your connections requires practice and kindness toward yourself. No one transforms overnight, and the journey involves making mistakes and learning from them rather than beating yourself up. When emotions spike, it's easy to feel ashamed or frustrated, especially if past patterns have kept you stuck in codependency or emotional fusion. Rather than spiraling into guilt, remind yourself that every step toward awareness is progress. With consistent effort, it becomes easier to respond rather than react, creating healthier dynamics over time.

Another important piece to managing triggers is understanding your partner's or loved one's triggers as well. When both sides take responsibility for their emotional regulation, the relationship becomes a space of mutual respect and patience. You don't have to fix the other person or control their feelings, but showing empathy and acknowledging their pain can de-escalate tension significantly. Sometimes just saying, "I see that this is hard for you," helps both parties feel heard and less alone in the moment.

Boundaries also play a crucial role in maintaining calm during challenging moments. Setting clear limits about what you can tolerate emotionally and behaviorally protects your well-being and reduces the chances of triggers causing damage. For some, this might mean taking a break during heated conversations, agreeing on how to communicate respectfully, or deciding when to seek outside support. Boundaries are acts of self-care that ultimately strengthen your connection because they foster trust and safety.

It's natural to want immediate solutions when someone you care about gets triggered. Yet, patience is key. Emotional regulation can't be forced—it's cultivated over time through consistency and compassion. Sometimes, the best response is quiet presence, allowing space for emotions to settle without judgment or interruption. When calm returns, conversations can happen with clearer minds and open hearts, which leads to deeper understanding and resolution.

Emotional regulation techniques, such as mindfulness and grounding, aren't just tools for crisis moments—they're daily practices that build resilience. Regularly tuning into your emotional state makes it easier to catch early signs of reactivity before they take hold. Imagine approaching conflict with curiosity instead of fear, or being able to pause and choose your words instead of reacting impulsively. That kind of control enriches all your relationships, not just romantic ones.

Sometimes triggers come from unexpected sources, including stress outside the relationship or internal self-judgment. Awareness of this fact can help prevent misdirected reactions. If you recognize that you're carrying tension from work or personal struggles, acknowledging this can prevent taking it out on someone you love. Developing a habit of checking in with yourself first allows for healthier interactions—where you can say, "I'm feeling overwhelmed right now; can we pause and reconnect later?" rather than unleashing frustration unintentionally.

Maintaining calm in connections doesn't mean suppressing your feelings or avoiding difficult conversations. On the contrary, it's about creating a container where emotions can be expressed safely and constructively. This requires vulnerability and trust—two pillars of interdependent relationships. When both partners feel safe sharing their triggers and struggles without fear of judgment or rejection, it deepens intimacy and fosters growth.

Managing triggers also includes practical preparation before entering potentially difficult conversations. Taking time to reflect on your emotional state and practicing calming strategies ahead of time can prime you for better responses. Visualizing how you want to show up or rehearsing phrases that communicate your needs clearly can reduce anxiety. Preparation is not about scripting every word but about setting your intention to remain grounded and respectful, no matter what unfolds.

It's worth noting that while managing your own triggers is vital, it's equally important to recognize when a relationship dynamic becomes harmful despite your best efforts. If you find yourself repeatedly triggered with little opportunity for resolution or growth, it might be time to reevaluate whether the connection supports your healing and well-being. Healthy relationships allow space for emotional regulation, not constant reactivity or emotional exhaustion.

Remember, triggers are not a sign of weakness; they're part of being human. Everyone has emotional vulnerabilities, and managing them skillfully is an essential part of building lasting, fulfilling connections. By increasing self-awareness, practicing calm, and setting boundaries that honor your needs, you take powerful steps toward healthy interdependence. Over time, what once felt like overwhelming emotional surges becomes manageable moments of insight and connection.

Ultimately, managing triggers and maintaining calm isn't about perfection. It's about commitment to growth and kindness—toward yourself and those you care about. When you nurture these habits, relationships transform from battlegrounds of reactivity into spaces where you can both feel safe, heard, and supported. That's the foundation for emotional freedom and a balanced, resilient partnership.

CHAPTER 9

WHAT INTERDEPENDENCE LOOKS LIKE IN PRACTICE

Interdependence in real life isn't about losing yourself or becoming overly reliant on someone else; it's a balanced dance where both people bring their wholeness to the relationship while still growing individually. It means trusting your partner and giving each other space to be who you truly are, without fear of abandonment or judgment. When practiced well, interdependence creates a foundation where emotional responsibility is shared—not piled onto one person—and where support feels freeing instead of binding. It looks like honest communication without fear, respect for boundaries that protect personal identity, and the courage to be vulnerable while maintaining a strong sense of self. This dynamic doesn't just happen; it requires conscious effort and a commitment to keep nurturing both connection and autonomy, so relationships become a source of strength, not codependence.

Healthy Connection Versus Emotional Merging Explained

When exploring what true interdependence looks like in real life, one of the most important distinctions to make is between a healthy connection and emotional merging. These two experiences can feel similar on the surface, especially early in relationships, but they represent fundamentally different dynamics. A healthy connection supports individuality, growth, and mutual respect, while emotional merging risks losing the boundaries that keep each person emotionally grounded and autonomous.

Healthy connection happens when two individuals come together as whole, separate people who choose to share their lives without trying to fill an inner void with the other. It's about joining without sacrificing one's sense of self. When people connect in this way, each partner maintains personal interests, beliefs, and emotional responsibilities. This kind of relationship creates a secure, supportive environment where both people can thrive independently, while still enjoying closeness and intimacy. There is emotional safety in knowing the bond is based on respect for each other's uniqueness, not on dependency or desperation.

Emotional merging, by contrast, occurs when the boundaries between partners blur or dissolve. Instead of feeling like two individuals who happen to share a connection, merging makes it hard to tell where one person ends and the other begins. This often looks like over-identification with a partner's feelings, needs, and struggles. Emotional fusion can create a powerful illusion of closeness, but it's one built on neediness and codependent patterns. In these dynamics, people often lose track of their own thoughts and feelings because they're so wrapped up in the emotional state of the other person. Over time, this breeds resentment, exhaustion, and disconnection despite the appearance of intimacy.

Understanding the difference between these two dynamics requires paying attention to boundaries—both emotional and psychological. Boundaries serve as a crucial guardrail ensuring that proximity doesn't turn into entanglement. When each person honors their internal limits, they stay attuned to their own feelings without taking on the burden of the other's emotions as their own. This creates space for empathy rather than emotional enmeshment. The ability to hold space for another's vulnerability without losing oneself is an essential skill in cultivating healthy interdependence.

One way to think about this is through the metaphor of a dance. In a healthy connection, two dancers maintain their own rhythm and movements, coordinating gracefully but not losing their individuality. Each person knows when to lead, when to follow, and when to step back. In emotional merging, however, the dancers' movements become tangled. There's confusion over who is moving who, and personal boundaries collapse. This can quickly feel overwhelming and suffocating, rather than liberating or energizing.

Emotional merging often stems from unconscious fears around abandonment and worthiness. People who grow up feeling unsafe or unheard may grab onto a partner as a way to validate their existence. This creates a cycle where emotional survival depends on constant connection and approval. What looks like love or deep bonding from the outside can actually be a pattern of extreme dependency. It's subtle, but the consequences are profound—losing touch with your true self, sacrificing your needs, and feeling perpetually anxious about the relationship's stability.

In contrast, a healthy connection encourages both partners to bring their full, authentic selves into the relationship. It allows for vulnerability without blame or pressure to fix, and it values honest communication about needs and limits. When you feel safe enough to say, "I need some time alone" or "I'm feeling overwhelmed," and your partner respects that, you're witnessing a dynamic built on trust and mutual respect. This also means both people can celebrate their individuality, engaging in personal growth that feeds into the relationship instead of draining it.

It's important to recognize that healthy connection doesn't mean being emotionally detached or distant. Interdependence lies at the balance point between isolation and fusion. It's the freedom to depend on your partner and be depended on, without losing your footing. Emotional merging blurs that line, leading people either to cling too tightly or withdraw completely out of exhaustion. When you find that middle ground, where you are connected yet separate, you build a relationship that's resilient and fulfilling.

One practical indicator of emotional merging is when one person consistently absorbs the other's emotional highs and lows as if they were their own. This goes beyond empathy—it's emotional over-involvement. If you notice yourself taking full responsibility for your partner's feelings or feel guilty for having separate emotions, you may be slipping into emotional merging. In healthy connections, partners can share feelings openly but still maintain emotional boundaries, acknowledging that each person is responsible for managing their inner world.

A key part of shifting from emotional merging to a healthy connection involves learning to tolerate healthy discomfort. Sometimes, being emotionally close means sitting with difficult feelings like frustration, sadness, or anger—without trying to smooth over or "fix" them immediately. Emotional merging seeks to eliminate discomfort at all costs, which can lead to avoidance of necessary confrontation or honest conversations. In contrast, healthy connection trusts that love is strong enough to weather these moments, allowing space for growth and healing.

Another difference lies in how decisions are made within the relationship. Emotional merging often shows up as codependent decision-making, where one person's needs overshadow the other's, or where decisions are made out of fear of upsetting the balance. Healthy connections prioritize collaborative decision-making that honors both partners' autonomy and preferences. This means being able to say no, express disagreement, or pursue individual interests without fearing emotional fallout.

It's also helpful to notice how self-care fits into these dynamics. In an emotionally merged relationship, self-care can feel selfish or disloyal. People might neglect their own mental, physical, or emotional health to keep the relationship functioning or to avoid conflict. On the other hand, healthy connection recognizes that self-care is essential—not just for individual well-being but for the vitality of the relationship itself. Partners who value themselves will inherently bring more energy, patience, and authenticity into their shared life.

Creating healthy interdependence requires practice and intentionality. It starts with self-awareness—understanding your emotional triggers, patterns of codependency, and fears around connection. It also involves learning new skills such as assertive communication, boundary-setting, and self-regulation. These tools build a foundation where both partners can meet each other as equals, each fully responsible for their own emotional reality.

One way to reinforce a healthy connection is by consciously embracing vulnerability without expectation. Vulnerability means allowing yourself to be seen—even your flaws and imperfections—without relying on your partner to "fix" or "rescue" you. When vulnerability is met with acceptance rather than judgment or emotional takeover, it strengthens trust and deepens intimacy. This builds a secure base from which both people can explore their individuality and shared life together.

It's natural to desire closeness and to want to feel deeply connected to those we love. The challenge lies in finding a way to meet that desire without sacrificing independence or falling into unhealthy patterns. Emotional merging can feel safe in the moment because it blurs the difficult boundaries of self, but it ultimately undermines long-term fulfillment.

On the other hand, healthy connection honors both the pull to be near and the need to be separate. It encourages growth on both individual and relational levels, providing a nourishing balance between autonomy and intimacy. This balance transforms relationships from a source of anxiety and codependency into a wellspring of support, inspiration, and joy.

In your journey toward interdependence, keep in mind that building healthy connections takes time, patience, and resilience. You'll likely face old patterns, setbacks, and moments of doubt. But each step toward clear boundaries, emotional responsibility, and self-acceptance brings you closer to the kind of relationship where both people feel free, valued, and deeply connected—without losing themselves in the process.

Trust, Space, and Emotional Responsibility in Relationships

In an interdependent relationship, trust isn't just a buzzword—it's the very foundation that allows both partners to thrive as individuals while growing together. Trust means believing in your partner's intentions, knowing they'll respect your boundaries, and feeling confident that you can rely on one another without losing your own sense of self. But building this kind of trust doesn't happen overnight. It requires consistent actions, honest communication, and the courage to be vulnerable without fear of judgment or abandonment.

Often, people caught in patterns of codependency confuse closeness with trust. They feel that constant togetherness equals security. On the surface, it might seem that way, but in reality, trust flourishes in an environment where both partners feel safe to have space—physical, emotional, and mental. This space allows each person to breathe, reflect, and maintain their identity. It prevents the unhealthy fusing of emotional needs that turns "we" into a tangled "me-and-you" where boundaries blur.

Giving space doesn't mean withdrawing love or interest. Rather, it's a powerful gift you give to a partner and to yourself. It says, "I trust that your individual growth and needs are just as important as our connection." In practice, this might look like encouraging your partner to pursue hobbies, spend time with friends alone, or simply have moments of quiet reflection. The same goes for you—cultivating your own interests and friendships keeps your identity intact and strengthens the relationship's emotional foundation.

But space and trust alone won't transform a relationship unless emotional responsibility is part of the deal. Emotional responsibility means owning your feelings without blaming or expecting your partner to fix what's inside you. It means recognizing that while your partner can support you, your emotional state is ultimately your own to manage. This doesn't imply shutting down or going through struggles in isolation. Instead, it's about expressing emotions honestly and respectfully, and then working toward understanding, healing, and growth independently and together.

In relationships riddled with codependency, people often feel overwhelmed by their partner's emotions or rely heavily on them to regulate how they feel. This creates a toxic feedback loop where emotional overwhelm is handed back and forth like a hot potato. Over time, this pattern leads to exhaustion, resentment, and a losing battle to preserve individuality. Interdependence turns this dynamic upside down by encouraging emotional autonomy. Each person becomes capable of recognizing and soothing their feelings, which in turn fosters empathy and genuine support without enmeshment.

Trust also opens the door for healthy conflict, which is essential in any strong relationship. When partners know they can experience emotional distance without abandoning each other, conflicts no longer feel like battles to win or threats to the relationship's survival. Instead, they become opportunities for deeper understanding and connection. Respecting space during disagreements means you can step back to cool down, reflect, and come back to the conversation more grounded and open. This ability to pause without panic is a sign of mature trust and emotional responsibility.

Another important aspect of trust and space is the allowance for imperfection. No partner—or relationship—is flawless. Interdependence means accepting each other with all the messiness that comes with being human, including mistakes, fears, and insecurities. It invites curiosity rather than judgment. When you trust your partner enough to reveal your vulnerabilities, and they respond with compassion instead of criticism, a new level of intimacy unfolds. This cycle strengthens the bond while respecting the personal boundaries that keep both people feeling safe and valued.

Maintaining emotional responsibility also requires self-awareness. You have to know yourself well enough to differentiate your feelings from your partner's and understand what situations trigger you. This level of insight takes practice and often involves reflecting on past experiences and patterns, sometimes from childhood or earlier adult relationships. It can be uncomfortable but is crucial for preventing emotional takeover. When you recognize these triggers, it's easier to take a breath, pause, and choose a response aligned with your values rather than reacting out of fear or resentment.

Space and trust also help counteract the tendency to people-please or overaccommodate in relationships. When you give yourself permission to have your own emotional experiences and needs, you naturally begin to say "no" without guilt or fear of disrupting the connection. Space acts as a buffer that allows you to honor your boundaries without guilt trips or emotional manipulation sneaking in. Because trust anchors the relationship, your partner can respect your limits without feeling rejected or attacked.

At the same time, these dynamics encourage active participation from both partners rather than passive dependence. Each person takes responsibility for their emotional health, which means seeking help when needed, using healthy coping mechanisms, and communicating needs clearly. This balance prevents one partner from carrying the entire emotional weight or bouncing between caretaking and withdrawing. Instead, you create a partnership where both people are emotionally equipped to offer genuine care and support.

When trust is solid, space is respected, and emotional responsibility is embraced, the relationship becomes a safe haven rather than a pressure cooker. You can share your deepest fears or greatest joys knowing your partner won't either dismiss or overwhelm you. This emotional rhythm fosters resilience, so setbacks or conflicts don't feel catastrophic but rather part of a shared journey toward growth.

One practical way to cultivate these qualities is through agreed-upon routines that honor space and check in on trust. Setting aside moments to ask, "How are we doing with our boundaries?" or "Do we feel safe sharing our feelings today?" keeps the relationship aligned and prevents misunderstanding from festering. These conversations help keep trust alive and prevent resentment from quietly building in the cracks of unmet needs.

Trust, space, and emotional responsibility are intertwined, each strengthening the others. Without trust, space feels like neglect. Without space, trust suffocates. Without emotional responsibility, both trust and space crumble under unexpressed needs and unresolved conflicts. Interdependence invites you to hold these elements in dynamic balance, creating relationships that bring freedom rather than confinement.

For those who've suffered through codependent patterns, embracing trust, space, and emotional responsibility might feel radical or even risky. That's understandable. Past wounds can make anyone wary of opening up or stepping back for fear of losing connection. The key is small steps—showing trust in little ways and creating pockets of space without pulling away completely. Over time, these actions become habits that rebuild the nervous system's sense of safety in relationships.

Emotional responsibility doesn't mean being perfect; it means being committed to growth. It means saying, "I messed up," or "I need time to process," instead of blaming or shutting down. It also means asking for what you need without expecting your partner to read your mind or fix everything. This shift honestly changes the tone of the entire relationship, allowing both partners to breathe and grow freely while staying connected.

In sum, trust, space, and emotional responsibility form the backbone of what interdependence really looks like in practice. They turn relationships into places where both people feel secure enough to be themselves and strong enough to face life's challenges together rather than losing themselves in each other. These principles act as a guiding light for stepping away from unhealthy enmeshment and toward loving partnerships that honor individuality, growth, and authentic connection.

CHAPTER 10

Communication That Deepens Intimacy

Building true intimacy requires more than just talking; it demands communication that fosters connection and trust by encouraging openness and vulnerability without fear of judgment. When you speak your needs clearly and assertively, you invite honesty and create a safe space where both partners feel valued and understood, which is essential in breaking free from codependent patterns. Equally important is the art of listening—really listening without defensiveness or interruption—so you can genuinely absorb your partner's perspective and emotions. This reciprocal exchange not only strengthens emotional bonds but also allows both individuals to maintain their sense of self while growing closer in a balanced, interdependent relationship. By practicing communication that prioritizes respect, empathy, and clarity, you lay the groundwork for intimacy that's deep, resilient, and transformative.

Speaking Your Needs Clearly and Assertively

When relationships start to deepen, many people find themselves stuck between fear of rejection and the desire to be truly understood. Speaking your needs clearly and assertively becomes essential not only for your own well-being but also for creating emotional safety and trust with your partner. For individuals recovering from codependency, this step can feel like uncharted territory. The habit of minimizing one's feelings or brushing aside personal needs to keep the peace might have been ingrained for years. But breaking out of this cycle is crucial. Without openly expressing what you need, the relationship risks slipping into resentment, misunderstanding, or emotional distance.

At its core, assertive communication isn't about demanding or controlling others. It's about owning your feelings and asking for what feels right to you with confidence and respect. When you speak with clarity and conviction, you send a powerful message: your emotions and boundaries matter. You are inviting your partner or loved one to step into a space where honesty and mutual respect thrive. This doesn't guarantee that others will always respond as you hope, but it dramatically increases the chances of being heard and valued authentically.

People who struggle with codependency often fear that stating their needs directly might lead to conflict, abandonment, or feelings of humiliation. These fears aren't unfounded—they come from real past experiences where expressing oneself may have led to punishment or neglect. That's why it's important to prepare yourself mentally before diving into assertive conversations. Practicing how to articulate your thoughts calmly and without apology can soften what initially feels like an intimidating challenge. The goal is to express your needs without shrinking or exaggerating, but with genuine clarity.

Confidence in clear communication doesn't happen overnight. It's a muscle you build through practice and patience. One way to start is by distinguishing the difference between passive, aggressive, and assertive communication. Passive communication often looks like avoidance or subtle hints—you might think someone will just "get it" if you don't say much. Aggressive communication, on the other hand, involves pushing your needs forcefully or disrespectfully, which can shut down dialogue and harm connection. Assertiveness strikes a middle ground where you're honest and direct but also open and respectful.

For example, instead of saying, "You never listen to me," which might provoke defensiveness, try, "I feel unheard when I don't get to finish my thoughts, and it's important for me to be listened to." See how the latter puts a spotlight on your feelings and needs rather than blaming the other person?

Statements like these—often called "I" statements—help keep conversations constructive and non-threatening.

Another critical factor in speaking your needs clearly is knowing exactly what those needs are. This requires self-awareness and reflection. Before entering a discussion, take a moment to check in with yourself. What do you truly want to convey? Are you seeking support, clarity, space, or reassurance? The clearer you are internally, the easier it will be to communicate externally. Regular journaling or quiet moments of introspection can help uncover patterns in your needs, making it simpler to express them the next time the opportunity arises.

It's also vital to recognize that assertive communication includes being ready for varied responses. Sometimes, even when you express yourself clearly, the other person may respond defensively or withdraw. This can feel disappointing, but it doesn't mean your needs aren't valid or that you've done something wrong. Part of developing emotional resilience within relationships is holding firm in your value—knowing your voice deserves to be heard regardless of immediate reactions. This strength shifts your sense of power from depending on others' approval to trusting your own truth.

Body language and tone of voice play a huge role when expressing needs. Even the clearest words can lose impact if delivered with hesitation or hostility. Maintaining steady eye contact, a calm yet confident tone, and open posture communicates sincerity and openness. If you notice your voice trembling or your words rushing, pause briefly, breathe, and ground yourself. These small adjustments help reinforce that you're centered and serious about your request, which tends to encourage more thoughtful responses from those listening.

In healthier interdependent relationships, speaking your needs assertively also helps dismantle unhealthy power dynamics. When one person habitually sacrifices their needs or stays silent to avoid conflict, it inadvertently creates imbalance. Over time, this imbalance breeds resentment and emotional disconnection. By stepping into clear self-expression, you co-create a relationship dynamic where both partners feel safe to share openly without fear of judgment or rejection. This mutual vulnerability is the foundation for deep intimacy that's both safe and thrilling.

Clear and assertive communication also means knowing when and where to speak your needs. Timing and environment matter. Important conversations deserve privacy and an undistracted setting. Trying to express something vulnerable in the heat of an argument or during a stressful moment can make it harder for all involved to listen and respond constructively. Recognizing the right moments to open up fosters better understanding and leads to more compassionate exchanges.

Equally important is practicing consistent honesty with yourself. Sometimes we avoid stating our needs due to shame or guilt—especially if those needs seem to contradict what we believe we 'should' want. Challenging internalized beliefs about self-worth or the fear of burdening others requires ongoing effort. Affirmations like "My needs are valid" or "I have the right to ask for what I need" can serve as grounding reminders during moments of doubt.

It's helpful to remember that assertiveness isn't just for romantic partnerships. The skills of expressing yourself clearly apply to family, friends, and even work relationships. Every connection benefits when there is transparent communication about needs and boundaries. As you grow more confident in your ability to speak assertively, you'll find that these skills ripple outward, improving interactions across all areas of life.

When you begin to practice speaking your needs clearly and assertively, start small. Identify something manageable to express—perhaps requesting help with a chore, or asking for a particular way to be supported during a tough day. Celebrate these small victories. Over time, as you build trust in your voice and in others' willingness to listen, you'll feel more empowered to share deeper, more vulnerable needs. This progress marks a healing journey away from codependency and toward authentic interdependence.

Finally, keep in mind that vulnerability and assertiveness are not opposites. True assertiveness often requires vulnerability—the courage to be seen and heard without an armor of anger or silence. When you combine clarity with a gentle openness, you invite connection rather than distance. Your needs become the bridge that strengthens the emotional bond, rather than the wedge that divides it.

Speaking your needs clearly and assertively is a revolutionary act for those who have endured codependent patterns. It's an act of self-love and courage that rewires old habits and reshapes relationship norms. By embracing this practice, you honor your authentic self and lay the groundwork for relationships that nourish both freedom and connection. This balance is the heartbeat of interdependence—a place where both individuals thrive together without losing their own voices.

Listening Without Defensiveness to Foster Understanding

Listening is one of those skills that seems deceptively simple until you actually try to do it well, especially within intimate relationships. When emotions run high, it's easy to slip into a defensive stance without even realizing it. Defensiveness shows up as interrupting, justifying, or mentally preparing a rebuttal instead of truly hearing what the other person is saying. This reaction, while understandable, can create a barrier to real connection and understanding.

Imagine for a moment that your partner is sharing something difficult. Maybe they're expressing hurt, frustration, or a concern. If your first instinct is to jump into defense mode—whether by minimizing their feelings or explaining your side right away—it sends an unintentional message: you're not safe to be fully seen. This shuts down authentic communication and, over time, deepens emotional distance. To break this cycle, listening without defensiveness isn't just helpful—it's essential for building intimacy that's grounded in trust and empathy.

At its core, listening without defensiveness means holding space for your partner's experience without reacting emotionally or physically shutting down. It requires patience and conscious effort. This doesn't mean you have to agree with everything said or surrender your perspective. Instead, it's about suspending judgment momentarily and resisting the urge to protect your ego or prove yourself right.

One of the biggest challenges is that defensiveness often stems from fear—fear of being misunderstood, blamed, or rejected. It can feel like a personal attack when someone points out a mistake or expresses dissatisfaction. But reframing the situation can be transformative. Instead of seeing feedback as a threat, view it as a gift—an invitation into your partner's inner world and a chance to grow closer. When you start to recognize this, the urge to defend diminishes.

So how does one develop this kind of listening? It begins by grounding yourself before the conversation even happens. Take a breath and remind yourself that your partner's feelings are valid, even if they don't align with your own perception. Set the intention to understand rather than respond. Active listening techniques can help here: nodding, maintaining eye contact, and reflecting back what you hear with phrases like "It sounds like you're feeling..." or "What I'm hearing is..." These gestures signal to your partner that they're truly being heard and not dismissed.

Another important piece is managing your internal dialogue. When feelings of defensiveness arise, notice them without reacting immediately. Ask yourself, "Why am I feeling this way right now? What am I afraid of?" Often, the root lies in wounds or insecurities from past experiences. By becoming aware of these triggers, you can separate your partner's message from your own fears, allowing an open heart to listen.

There's also a powerful difference between hearing and listening. Hearing happens passively—your ears pick up sounds but your mind might be elsewhere. Listening, on the other hand, requires presence and engagement. You are fully there with the person speaking, not mentally rehearsing your comeback or distracted by outside stressors. This level of attention fosters trust, showing your partner that their voice matters deeply to you.

Of course, listening without defensiveness doesn't guarantee that conversations will always be easy or conflict-free. Sometimes the truth hurts. But it creates a safer emotional environment where vulnerability can flourish. When both partners practice this form of attentive listening, it becomes easier to express needs, boundaries, or disappointments without fear of immediate shutdown or escalation.

Keep in mind, it's normal to struggle with this skill, especially at first. Old patterns can be tenacious, and reactive defensiveness might pop up unexpectedly. The key is to recognize when it happens and gently redirect. Apologizing for moments when you did react defensively can open doors for further dialogue and healing. It shows humility and a commitment to growth that your partner is likely to appreciate.

Another technique to support listening without defensiveness is to pause when receiving difficult feedback. A simple, "I want to understand you better—can you tell me more about that?" invites elaboration and slows down the emotional charge. Sometimes just holding space for silence can disarm tension and encourage deeper exploration rather than surface-level reactions.

In relationships marked by codependency, this practice can be even more important. When blurred boundaries and fear of abandonment are involved, defensiveness might often be a defensive shield around fragile self-esteem. Letting go of this shield takes courage and vulnerability. However, by doing so, you pave the way for mutual respect and emotional safety, which are the foundation stones of interdependence.

Integrating compassionate listening also means balancing your own needs with your partner's. It's not about absorbing all the blame or feeling responsible for fixing the problem on your own. Instead, it's recognizing that understanding someone else's experience isn't about winning or being right—it's about connection. When you listen without defensiveness, you're affirming that connection, creating a dialogue that moves beyond blame and toward solutions.

Learning this skill requires practice, patience, and sometimes support from outside resources like therapy or communication workshops. But the impact on your relationships—whether with romantic partners, family members, or friends—can be profound. You begin to notice more openness, less conflict, and a greater sense of being seen and accepted for who you are.

Remember, fostering understanding is a two-way street. While you work on your listening, encourage your partner to do the same. Cultivating a shared commitment to non-defensive communication turns challenges into opportunities. When both people feel safe to express and receive feedback openly, intimacy naturally deepens, forming a bond resistant to old patterns of codependency.

Finally, practicing listening without defensiveness is a radical act of self-love and love for your partner. It requires setting aside ego and pride in favor of curiosity and empathy. But the reward is well worth the effort. You create a space where both individuals can grow, heal, and thrive together—free from cycles of blame and misunderstanding.

CHAPTER 11

Loving Without Losing Yourself

Loving someone deeply doesn't mean you have to disappear or forget who you are; in fact, preserving your identity is essential to building a relationship that thrives on genuine connection rather than dependency. When you maintain your passions, values, and boundaries, you create a space where both partners can grow individually while supporting each other mutually. It's about striking a balance between sharing your true self and remaining open to change, without surrendering your sense of autonomy. This approach not only protects your emotional well-being but also fosters a healthier, more resilient bond where love enhances rather than consumes.

Staying grounded in yourself allows you to love freely, with presence and purpose, breaking free from the patterns that once kept you lost in others.

Maintaining Identity Within Partnership

When two people come together in a relationship, it's natural to want to connect deeply—and yet, maintaining your own sense of self is vital. Without preserving your individuality, love risks becoming a fusion where boundaries blur, and personal needs get overshadowed. This section explores how you can stay grounded in your identity while building a meaningful partnership that supports growth, intimacy, and freedom.

One of the biggest challenges for many people is resisting the pull to lose themselves when they fall in love. Often, the desire to be loved and accepted can lead to self-sacrifice or codependent behaviors, where one's happiness becomes too entangled with the partner's approval or emotions. This often starts subtly—small compromises that feel harmless at first but accumulate. Over time, you might find that your interests fade, your opinions soften, and your goals become less visible, swallowed by the relationship dynamic. Recognizing this is the first step to correcting course.

Maintaining identity within partnership means consciously holding space for who you are, independent of your partner. It's about staying connected to your passions, values, and beliefs even as you share your life with someone else. For instance, maintaining hobbies, friendships, and personal rituals preserves your autonomy. These aren't acts of rebellion or disconnection; rather, they're essential expressions of self-respect and emotional health. When you nurture yourself, both you and your relationship benefit.

It's critical to understand that identity doesn't mean isolation or distance—it's about balance. Healthy interdependent relationships thrive when two people bring their whole selves, not halves. Imagine your relationship as a dance where each partner moves independently yet harmonizes beautifully. When you stay true to your identity, you contribute in a more authentic, confident way, allowing your partner to do the same. This creates a dynamic where connection feels enriching, not consuming.

One practical way to maintain your identity is through regular self-reflection. Carving out time for journaling, meditation, or simple quiet moments helps you check in with your feelings, desires, and boundaries. These pauses remind you of your priorities and help you spot when you're slipping into patterns of over-giving or people-pleasing to keep the peace. Relationship stress can sometimes numb your own voice if you let it, so actively tuning in keeps your inner compass intact.

Boundaries also play a crucial role in supporting your identity. Setting limits about how much time and energy you devote to the relationship or requests you honor might feel uncomfortable at first—especially if you're used to pleasing others. However, boundaries are a form of self-care, demonstrating to both you and your partner that your needs matter. Saying no when something doesn't feel right isn't rejection; it's an honest declaration of your presence as a whole person.

You might notice that maintaining identity sometimes invites conflict or discomfort. This is normal. When you assert your needs or preferences, your partner might push back, especially if they're used to a different dynamic. This can stir fears of abandonment or rejection, but resisting these fears is part of the journey. Emotional maturity in relationships grows as both partners learn to hold space for differences without seeing them as threats. Over time, this acceptance deepens trust and respect.

It's also important to develop a strong relationship with yourself outside of your romantic connection. Your self-worth shouldn't depend solely on how well your relationship is going. Cultivating confidence in your own capabilities, achievements, and values nourishes your sense of identity. When you bring this inner strength to your partnership, you're less likely to compromise your core or lose yourself in the process of loving another.

One key pitfall to watch out for is emotional fusion—the tendency to feel responsible for your partner's feelings or to sync too closely with their emotional states. While empathy is a beautiful aspect of connection, losing the ability to distinguish where you end and your partner begins can erode your identity. Practice recognizing your emotions separately from your partner's, and allow space for each person to handle their own experiences. This doesn't mean growing cold or detached; instead, it fosters emotional resilience and mutual support.

Communication is another linchpin for maintaining identity within partnership. Being able to express your needs, boundaries, and perspectives honestly yet respectfully allows you to stay visible in the relationship. When you speak up, you invite your partner into your world, enriching the partnership rather than shrinking yourself to fit an imagined mold. Listening plays an equal role here; actively hearing your partner without defensiveness creates fertile ground for both of you to be yourselves.

In long-term partnerships, identity maintenance requires ongoing effort. Life changes like career shifts, family dynamics, or personal growth spur re-evaluation of what individuality means within the relationship. Partners who commit to continuous self-exploration and mutual support find that their connection evolves without losing sight of each other's unique identities. This kind of partnership often becomes a source of strength and freedom rather than constraint.

When you actively maintain your identity, you're also modeling an important message: that love doesn't demand losing yourself. This can empower your partner to do the same, fostering a healthy cycle of mutual growth. Rather than feeling locked or obligated, you both experience the relationship as a conscious choice made from strength and clarity. Interdependence blossoms when two secure and whole people deliberately choose to connect.

Another important aspect is resisting the urge to conform to your partner's expectations or societal pressures at the expense of your authenticity. Sometimes, cultural or familial influences frame "successful partnerships" in ways that promote merging or sacrificing individual dreams. Recognizing these external pressures helps you identify when you're acting out of fear or conditioning rather than genuine desire. Reclaiming your identity might involve gently but firmly pushing back on these narratives.

Finally, celebrate your individuality as a source of richness within the relationship instead of a threat. Your unique experiences, quirks, and perspectives add depth and color to your shared life. Embracing your authentic self invites your partner to do the same, amplifying connection and joy. Loving without losing yourself is not a contradiction; it's a beautiful dance that honors both union and autonomy.

In summary, maintaining identity within partnership means prioritizing your sense of self as you connect deeply with another. It involves setting boundaries, practicing honest communication, nurturing your inner life, and resisting emotional fusion. This balance creates a relationship defined not by loss, but by mutual support and freedom. When you can bring your full self to love, you create a foundation for resilience, peace, and lasting fulfillment.

Sharing Growth Without Sacrificing Autonomy

In interdependent relationships, the goal isn't just growing together but also preserving your individual identity. It's a delicate dance—two people moving in harmony without losing the very qualities that make them who they are. Often, when growth is shared, one partner may feel overshadowed or swallowed whole by the other's change, leading to subtle erosion of autonomy. The key is to cultivate a dynamic where both partners can evolve without blurring the lines that define them as unique individuals.

This balance starts with recognizing that personal growth does not require sacrificing your freedom or sense of self. In fact, sharing your development with someone else can be one of the most enriching experiences—if approached with intention and respect. When each person values their own journey as much as they honor their partner's, the relationship becomes a safe space to explore, experiment, and expand, all while maintaining solid boundaries. It's not about merging into one indistinguishable entity but rather about building a shared ecosystem that nourishes each person's well-being.

One practical way to prevent loss of autonomy during shared growth is to maintain clear self-awareness. Take time to check in with yourself regularly—what are your wants, needs, and limits? What aspects of your identity do you fiercely protect and nurture? When you stay connected to your core values and passions, it becomes much easier to participate in your partner's growth without losing sight of your own. This self-awareness also acts as a compass, guiding you when it feels like your individuality is slipping away.

It's common for people to confuse closeness with dependence, but closeness does not have to mean clinging. You can let your partner witness your growth without merging into their trajectory. Think of it this way: you each hold your own map, walking paths side by side. Sometimes the routes intersect, sometimes they don't, but what matters most is that you're both moving forward authentically. In this scenario, your autonomy isn't a threat to your connection; it's what keeps the relationship nutritious and vibrant.

Another important factor is communication. Honest and ongoing dialogue about your evolving needs helps prevent misunderstandings that could trigger feelings of losing control or self. Sharing your personal growth goals—and encouraging your partner to do the same—helps set mutual expectations. For example, you might want to take on new hobbies, spend time alone for reflection, or pursue career changes. When communicated clearly, your partner can offer support without feeling excluded or disrespected. Likewise, they might have needs that require similar accommodation from you. The goal is to create a space where growth conversations are welcomed rather than feared.

Supporting each other's development also means honoring boundaries around autonomy. While it can be tempting to dive headfirst into your partner's world, remember that true interdependence respects limits. If you feel pressured to conform or abandon aspects of yourself to keep peace or please your partner, that's a red flag. Healthy sharing of growth means both of you feel safe to say no, to prioritize personal time, and to protect your emotional and mental space. Boundaries don't push people apart; they actually create the conditions needed for connection to deepen.

It's vital to cultivate practices that anchor your identity during this process. What are daily or weekly rituals that root you in your individuality? Maybe it's a solo walk, journaling, or creative projects done independently. These rituals act like lifelines, helping you reconnect with your inner world amid the push and pull of relationship dynamics. When each partner maintains these practices, the relationship benefits. You'll bring more energy, clarity, and enthusiasm into shared spaces when you haven't lost your footing from leaning too hard on the other person.

Growth within relationships sometimes triggers fears—fear of abandonment, fear of being left behind, or fear of change itself. These fears can make autonomy feel risky, even dangerous. But leaning into autonomy actually cultivates trust between partners. It signals that you're stable enough on your own and confident enough in the relationship to allow space for personal transformation. Trust grows not only from closeness but also from knowing your partner respects your individuality. That respect, in turn, strengthens the commitment and intimacy you share.

There's also empowerment in mutual growth without losing autonomy. When both partners celebrate their personal achievements—without overshadowing or diminishing one another—it fosters a culture of shared success rather than competition. It's a chance to let each other shine in your unique ways and to find joy in those differences. Imagine a relationship where your partner cheering you on feels as natural as breathing, and where you do the same for them, understanding that your victories enhance the bond instead of weaken it.

In this context, autonomy becomes a gift, not a barrier. It helps prevent the classic trap of emotional fusion, where partners become so enmeshed that they lose clarity about who drives their growth and who is simply echoing the other. Maintaining autonomy ensures your growth is authentic and self-motivated. It's your journey first, and your partner's journey first. Together, those individual paths weave a stronger shared story over time rather than one partner subsuming the other.

Sometimes, sharing growth requires recalibrating your relationship rhythm. Growth spurts don't always line up neatly, and one person might be pushing forward while the other is holding steady or even taking a step back. That's okay. Respecting these fluctuations is part of sharing without sacrificing autonomy. It means supporting your partner's pace without forcing them to match yours, and asking for support when you need it without guilt. This kind of flexibility acknowledges that autonomy doesn't mean isolation; it means being free to travel your own road, with the comfort of knowing your partner respects your pace.

Finally, it's worth remembering that maintaining autonomy while sharing growth is a skill you develop over time. It requires patience, self-compassion, and practice. You'll encounter moments when boundaries blur, where old codependent patterns sneak back in, or where fear tempts you to cling too tightly. These moments don't mean failure—they're just signals that you need to pause, reflect, and reset. Each time you recommit to balancing closeness with independence, you reinforce the foundation of a healthier, more resilient relationship.

Ultimately, sharing growth without sacrificing autonomy doesn't just protect your sense of self—it elevates your relationship to a place where love feels expansive rather than confining. It's a powerful reminder that you can give deeply to another person while staying unapologetically true to yourself. When both partners embrace this truth, their connection becomes not only sustainable but truly transformative.

CHAPTER 12

WHEN THEY DON'T WANT TO CHANGE

It's incredibly painful when someone you care about resists change, especially when that change could lead to healthier, more balanced relationships. You might feel caught between hope and frustration, wanting to support them but realizing that transformation has to come from their own willingness. It's important to recognize that you can't force growth in others, no matter how much you wish for it; your energy is best spent on maintaining your own boundaries and emotional resilience. Facing this reality means making tough choices about how much you invest emotionally and whether staying in the dynamic serves your well-being. Growth doesn't happen on someone else's timeline, and learning to accept that can be a powerful step toward reclaiming your freedom and building the interdependent relationships you deserve.

How to Cope with Resistance in a Partner

Facing resistance from a partner who seems unwilling to change can be one of the toughest challenges in a relationship. It's common to feel stuck in a place where your desire for growth and healing meets your partner's closed door. The reality is that change has to come from within, and pushing or forcing it usually backfires. So, learning how to manage that resistance—without losing yourself or sacrificing your emotional health—is crucial.

When you encounter resistance, the first step is to acknowledge that your partner's reluctance or refusal to change doesn't reflect your worth or the value of your needs. Resistance often stems from fear, discomfort, or deeply ingrained patterns that can't be shifted overnight. It's important not to take their unwillingness personally or let it shake your sense of self. Your emotional well-being depends on recognizing that change is a choice your partner must make on their own timeline, even if that timeline is frustratingly slow or unclear.

That said, coping with resistance doesn't mean sitting back and accepting everything as it is. It requires a balance between compassion and firmness. Compassion helps you understand where your partner might be coming from—their fears, insecurities, or past wounds that make change feel threatening. But firmness means holding your boundaries and upholding your own growth, regardless of their current state. This balance fosters an environment where you can protect your emotional space while remaining open-hearted.

One helpful approach is to shift your focus inward. Instead of spending excessive energy trying to change your partner, redirect that energy toward cultivating your own emotional independence and resilience. This doesn't just benefit you; it models healthy behavior and can sometimes inspire gentle curiosity or willingness in your partner over time. Remember, growth often happens in unexpected ways, and your steady commitment to your own healing can act as a beacon rather than a battleground.

Communication plays a vital role here, but it requires tact and timing. When resistance is palpable, it's usually counterproductive to engage in confrontations that push for change directly. Instead, aim for conversations that express your feelings and needs clearly but without blame or pressure. Using "I" statements and focusing on your experience can reduce defensiveness and create a safer space for dialogue. For example, saying "I feel distant when we avoid talking about these things" opens a door without demanding your partner step through immediately.

At the same time, be prepared for the possibility that your partner may not respond as you hope. That's understandably disappointing and painful. It's natural to grieve the loss of the relationship you imagined—one where both partners grow together. Allow yourself the space to process those feelings without judgment, recognizing that grief doesn't weaken your strength.

It can also help to redefine what "change" looks like in your relationship. Instead of expecting dramatic shifts or immediate breakthroughs, celebrate small steps and moments of self-awareness that your partner might express, even if they don't appear consistent. Change is rarely a straight line; it's often a series of small movements forward and backward. Patience in this reality is not about passivity—it's about steady presence and realistic hope without sacrificing your own progress.

Coping with resistance means setting clear and loving boundaries about what you are willing to tolerate and what is non-negotiable for your mental and emotional health. Boundaries might include limits on how much you engage in specific conflicts or the choice to pause discussions that become hostile or dismissive. Healthy boundaries are not threats or punishments; they're self-care tools that maintain your dignity and encourage accountability.

Another vital tool for coping is community and support. Facing resistance alone can be isolating and exhausting. Seek out friendships, support groups, or a therapist who understands the dynamics of codependency and interdependence. These connections provide emotional validation and fresh perspectives, reminding you that your experience is real and that support is available beyond your partner.

It's equally essential to cultivate self-compassion. Resistance can trigger feelings of insecurity or self-doubt, tempting you to blame yourself or minimize your needs just to keep the peace. Instead, remind yourself regularly that your feelings are valid and that your commitment to a healthier relationship pattern is courageous. Self-compassion fuels resilience, helping you to stay grounded when your partner's behavior feels frustrating or disheartening.

Many people caught in this dynamic find themselves over-functioning—taking on more emotional responsibility than they should in hopes of easing their partner's resistance. While it's natural to want to support your loved one, this dynamic often reinforces unhealthy patterns. Learning to step back and resist the urge to fix or rescue can feel uncomfortable but is essential for both partners' growth. Change rarely happens through caretaking; it happens through personal responsibility.

Sometimes, resistance in a partner can lead to moments of confusion or second-guessing your path forward. It's normal to ask yourself, "Am I expecting too much?" or "Can this relationship really work if they won't change?" These are important questions. Clarifying what you need to feel respected and loved—and whether those needs are met—is part of managing resistance. It might mean reconsidering certain boundaries, or in some cases, making the difficult choice to step away if the resistance becomes damaging.

Ultimately, coping with resistance is about holding two truths simultaneously: you want your partner to grow, and you deserve a partnership where growth is possible and supported. Maintaining this perspective grounds your efforts in reality instead of frustration or denial. This dual awareness helps you stay aligned with your core values while accepting what is and isn't within your control.

It's also useful to remember that growth and healing often involve cycles of resistance and acceptance—both in our partners and in ourselves. While your partner may resist now, the relationship between you remains a living system that can evolve. Your role is not to force change but to embody the stable, loving presence that invites change when your partner is ready. This might mean stepping into patience and uncertainty, trusting in your own strength and capacity to thrive regardless of another's readiness.

Ultimately, learning to cope with resistance in a partner empowers you to take charge of your own healing journey rather than getting entangled in the frustration of unmet expectations. It builds emotional maturity and sets the foundation for healthier connections, whether with your current partner or in future relationships where mutual growth and respect become the norm.

In making peace with resistance, you create space for your own freedom. Your growth is not contingent on your partner's willingness. By facing resistance with compassion, boundaries, self-care, and realistic hope, you nurture a form of love that honors both your partner's humanity and your own unshakable value.

Making Hard Decisions from a Place of Personal Strength

When someone you care about refuses to change, it shakes you to your core. You want things to get better—you want growth, healing, and mutual support—but the resistance can feel like hitting an immovable wall. It's a deeply frustrating and painful place to be, especially if you've invested a lot of yourself emotionally. But amidst that struggle, the most important thing you can do is ground yourself in your own personal strength. Making hard decisions from this place is the key to preserving your well-being and paving the way toward healthier relationships.

Strength doesn't mean brute force or harshness. Instead, it's a quiet, steady foundation of self-respect, clarity, and inner resolve. It's about knowing your worth so well that decisions aren't motivated by fear, desperation, or the hope that someone else might just "wake up" and change. That kind of hope often keeps people stuck, tangled in codependent cycles where their needs become secondary to the struggle of trying to fix another person. True strength shifts the focus back to you and your journey.

At first, this can feel daunting. How do you decide when to stay and when to walk away—especially if you've invested years, shared dreams, or built a life together? You're not expected to have all the answers overnight. The process is messy and nonlinear, but starting from a place of personal power changes the narrative. You take the reins of your life, rather than letting the other person's unwillingness or resistance dictate your emotional landscape.

One of the most powerful steps is to get clear about your values and boundaries. What kind of relationship do you want? What behaviors are absolutely nonnegotiable? Defining these for yourself—even if it feels uncomfortable—grounds your decisions in integrity rather than reaction. You learn to say no without guilt because you understand that protecting your emotional health isn't selfish; it's necessary.

Sometimes people feel trapped by loyalty or obligation, especially when there's a shared history or family involved. These bonds are important, but they don't justify sacrificing your well-being for someone else's refusal to change. Making hard decisions rooted in strength means honoring those connections compassionately while recognizing where you need to draw a firm line. It's important not to confuse love with tolerating harm or stagnation.

There's a difference between supporting someone through their challenges and enabling destructive patterns. If you've tried repeatedly to encourage growth without any reciprocal effort, insisting on change at your own expense, you're likely sinking deeper into codependent behaviors. Strength is choosing to step back when your involvement no longer fosters healthy growth—sometimes for their sake as much as yours.

It's not easy to detach yourself emotionally in these situations. The instinct to fix or rescue can feel overpowering, fueled by fear of loss or loneliness. But leaning into your personal strength means accepting the reality of the other person's limitations without internalizing it as a reflection of your value or as a personal failure. This mindset shift is crucial for healing and moving forward with dignity.

Decision-making from strength also involves giving yourself permission to prioritize your emotional safety. This may mean initiating space—whether physical or emotional—to reassess what's best for you. Distance can provide much-needed perspective and allow both parties the opportunity to grow independently if change is going to happen at all. It's not about punishing or withdrawing love but about honoring your needs honestly.

Keep in mind that setting limits doesn't mean closing the door forever. Sometimes, those hard decisions carve out room for new possibilities, whether in the form of healthier interaction or, if necessary, different paths forward. You hold the power to define what engagement looks like on your terms, not theirs. And that autonomy is liberating.

Another key aspect of making these tough calls is self-compassion. Strength isn't about pushing yourself to be stoic or unfeeling. It's okay to acknowledge your pain, loss, or frustration. Allow yourself to grieve what might have been as you recalibrate your expectations. Being honest about your emotions fuels authenticity and resilience rather than denial or repression.

Surrounding yourself with support—whether from trusted friends, therapists, or support groups—can reinforce your resolve. Others who understand the challenges of codependency and emotional resistance provide encouragement and perspective, reminding you that you're not alone in this journey. Their insight can bolster your confidence as you navigate complicated feelings and decisions.

Remember, personal strength over time grows from consistent practice. Each small choice to uphold your boundaries, each moment of self-honesty, and every step away from unhealthy patterns builds your foundation. It's not a one-time event but an ongoing process. Patience with yourself and the unfolding situation nurtures endurance.

Sometimes the hardest decisions might involve ending a relationship that no longer serves your growth. This act, though painful, is often the clearest expression of self-love. Recognizing your courage in doing so reframes the narrative—not as failure but as empowerment. Choosing yourself in this way sends a powerful message that your worth cannot be compromised by someone else's refusal to meet you halfway.

At the heart of making hard decisions from personal strength lies a fundamental truth: you have the right to pursue a life filled with respect, partnership, and genuine connection. You don't have to settle for emotional stagnation or imbalance, no matter how much you wish things were different. Embracing this reality frees you from the exhausting burden of trying to fix what's not willing to change.

Ultimately, this journey teaches that freedom and healing don't come from others; they come from cultivating inner strength. When you anchor your decisions in that strength, you reclaim your power to shape a healthier future—one where relationships enhance your life instead of draining it. This is the true gift that arises on the other side of resistance and unmet expectations.

CHAPTER 13

DATING AFTER CODEPENDENCY

Stepping back into the dating world after codependency can feel both hopeful and daunting, but it's an essential part of reclaiming your emotional independence and building interdependent connections that honor your growth. It's about learning to recognize healthy red flags early on, trusting your instincts without letting past fears cloud your judgment, and embracing relationships where mutual respect and conscious awareness guide every interaction. This journey asks you to slow down, stay present, and make choices that reflect your worth—not out of need or fear, but from a genuine desire to connect authentically. Remember, dating is no longer about losing yourself in another person; it's about choosing someone who walks alongside you, respecting your boundaries and celebrating your individuality every step of the way.

Healthy Red Flags to Watch For in New Relationships

Stepping into the dating world after breaking free from codependency presents a unique set of challenges and opportunities. One critical skill that often takes time to develop is learning how to spot healthy red flags early in new relationships. These red flags don't mean danger or warning signs in the traditional sense; instead, they're subtle indicators that something important needs your attention—a chance to pause, reflect, and decide if this connection aligns with your values and emotional well-being.

After years of sacrificing your needs and boundaries, recognizing these subtle cues can feel like reclaiming a vital sense of self-protection. It's about tuning into your instincts and emotions in ways you might not have done before. Healthy red flags act as gentle reminders that a relationship isn't a smooth ride all the time, and that's okay. What matters is how you and your partner navigate those bumps together. Being mindful of these signals helps you avoid slipping back into old patterns of emotional fusion or people-pleasing.

One of the first healthy red flags to observe is how you feel when expressing your needs or opinions. It might seem simple, but feeling safe enough to share what's important to you without fear of rejection or judgment is a significant sign. If you notice moments where you hesitate, shrink, or censor yourself, that's a prompt to slow things down. Not because your needs are unreasonable, but because the environment might not fully support your emotional authenticity yet. A healthy red flag here might be a growing awareness that your feelings deserve space at the table.

Another red flag worth paying attention to is how your potential partner responds to your boundaries. Boundaries are foundational in creating balance—after all, they're the invisible lines that protect your emotional health. If your partner acknowledges your boundaries without frustration or attempts to test them, it's a nurturing signal. However, if you notice them reacting with impatience, guilt-tripping, or attempts to circumvent your limits, this discrepancy becomes a red flag. Healthy relationships require mutual respect for personal space, time, and emotional limits negotiated openly.

It's also essential to observe the way conflict emerges and is handled. Conflict isn't an indicator of failure; rather, it can be a canvas where true connection too many times gets painted. Healthy red flags reveal themselves in how disagreements are met—not through escalation, avoidance, or manipulation, but with genuine curiosity and respect. You might feel heard, even if you don't agree on everything. Healthy communication around conflict fosters trust and deepens intimacy, so any hint that conversations turn dismissive or hostile should be noted as a sign to reflect carefully.

Paying attention to the pace of the relationship can be incredibly revealing, too. There's a natural rhythm that develops between people who have healthy emotional availability. If you find yourself being rushed into hyper-intimacy or pressured to move faster than you feel comfortable with, this is a subtle but crucial red flag. Good relationships thrive on a balance between closeness and space, where both individuals can maintain their identities alongside shared growth. Your comfort with how quickly things unfold is a compass worth trusting.

Genuine interest in your whole self—not just the parts you present on a surface level—is another key area to watch. Healthy red flags often show up as your partner's curiosity about your history, dreams, struggles, and strengths without rushing to fix or judge you. When someone approaches your story with empathy instead of trying to "save" you or change who you are, it creates a fertile ground for interdependence. On the other hand, if their interest feels conditional or self-serving, that's a red flag that shouldn't be overlooked.

A frequent pitfall for those healing from codependency involves confusing intense emotional displays for deep connection. Healthy red flags in new relationships ask you to distinguish between passionate bursts of drama and steady, consistent warmth. If you notice highs and lows that leave you emotionally drained or anxious, pay attention. While all relationships have ups and downs, a steady sense of support and emotional availability points to healthier terrain. Trustworthy partners offer reliability even when life gets messy.

Watch too for how your growing relationship integrates with your existing support systems. If a new partner is respectful and encouraging of your friendships, family ties, and personal interests, it's a healthy sign. Those who try to isolate you or sow doubt about your loved ones generally trigger unhealthy dynamics. Healthy red flags show up as inclusive attitudes that motivate self-growth and balanced social connections. Navigating life together doesn't require cutting off your past or support networks—it enriches your presence in both worlds.

Financial boundaries can also carry important clues. While money often carries stigma or feels taboo to discuss early on, noticing how money conversations arise can provide insights into respect and equality within the partnership. Healthy red flags might include openness and transparency even if the topic feels uncomfortable at first. If money becomes a source of control, secrecy, or manipulation, that's a significant indicator to reconsider. Honesty about finances signals a foundation for trust and shared responsibility.

Empathy—feeling your partner's emotions without losing yourself—is an advanced but vital healthy red flag. Early in a relationship, this may appear as thoughtful gestures or simply sensing when your partner is struggling without them having to spell it out. However, empathy in this context isn't just about emotional attunement but also about balancing care for the other with care for yourself. If you find that providing emotional support leaves you hollow or fearful of your own needs being overlooked, that dynamic needs scrutiny.

Humor and lightheartedness are often underrated but powerful healthy red flags. Sharing laughter and play supports emotional resilience and generates positive cycles of connection. When you can relax, be silly, or enjoy small moments together without pressure or fear, it deeply signals healthy compatibility.

Conversely, if the mood feels tense or overly serious all the time, it might highlight underlying mismatches in how you both handle stress and joy.

Expectations and future planning also deserve your attention. When your partner openly discusses hopes and goals, even in early stages, it creates room for aligned visions. Healthy red flags include conversations about autonomy within shared dreams—supporting each other's ambitions while respecting individuality. If future talks get shut down abruptly or met with hostility, it could mean a deeper incompatibility with your growth path. Healthy connections allow space to dream both together and independently.

Perhaps one of the most important red flags relates directly to your inner voice. Sometimes the most obvious warnings come in subtle emotional nudges—unease, hesitation, or feelings of disconnection. Developing attunement to these inner signals is crucial post-codependency. Your intuition often recognizes red flags before logic can parse them fully. Honoring these feelings doesn't require immediate decisions but invites you to pause, journal, or discuss your concerns with trusted confidantes. Over time, this practice strengthens your decision-making muscle, guiding you toward healthier relationships.

It's important, too, to pay attention to patterns rather than isolated incidents. One off day or minor misunderstanding is normal, but recurring themes that trigger old insecurities or boundaries deserve closer scrutiny. Healthy red flags reflect not just the actions of your partner but also how those actions impact your healing journey. Sometimes, a red flag points less to blame and more to an opportunity—for you both to grow or to recognize fundamental differences.

In the end, healthy red flags act less as stop signs and more as invitations to deepen your self-awareness and communication. They help you stay grounded in your personal value and needs as you flirt with vulnerability and intimacy again. Because dating after codependency isn't about perfection—it's about learning to love with open eyes and a courageous heart, knowing when to lean in and when to press pause for self-care.

As you navigate new connections, remember that healthy red flags are tools, not judgments. They help you maintain balance, foster mutual respect, and nurture relationships that don't demand losing yourself. Trusting these signals equips you to build partnerships rooted in interdependence—a place where you can both grow freely, support fiercely, and love authentically.

Creating Conscious and Mutual Connections

Stepping into the dating world after healing from codependency means approaching relationships with a new level of awareness and intention. It's a delicate balance between protecting yourself and remaining open to genuine connection. This stage isn't about rushing to fill a void or seeking validation from others, but rather about cultivating relationships based on mutual respect, understanding, and choice. When we talk about creating conscious and mutual connections, the emphasis is on awareness—being fully present with yourself and the other person—and on reciprocity, where both partners contribute to and benefit from the relationship equally.

For those who've struggled with codependency, this might feel unfamiliar territory. You may find yourself doubting your ability to engage in connections free from old patterns like people-pleasing or losing your boundaries. That's expected. Building conscious connections requires stepping out of automatic responses and learning to tune in to your needs and feelings, rather than instinctively prioritizing someone else's comfort over your own. It's a gradual process that calls for patience and persistent self-reflection.

One key to conscious connection is emotional honesty. This means being truthful with yourself first—acknowledging what you really want and feel instead of what feels safe or expected. Once you gain clarity internally, sharing those feelings becomes an act of courage rather than a risk. When you express yourself authentically, without fear of judgment or rejection, you invite the other person to do the same. This sets a foundation where emotional safety blooms—a core ingredient for any healthy, enduring relationship.

Mutuality is the other side of the coin, and it often poses a challenge for anyone recovering from codependency. After years of giving excessively and disregarding your own needs, it can feel strange to ask for what you want or to expect your partner to show up for you in a balanced way. Yet, mutual connections require give and take—a dance of independence and togetherness where both people feel seen, heard, and valued equally. This isn't just about compromise; it's about partnership. Each person brings their vulnerabilities, strengths, and boundaries to the relationship, and both are honored without sacrificing individuality.

Sometimes, people recovering from codependency confuse mutuality with selfishness. It's important to remember that prioritizing your feelings and boundaries doesn't mean being self-centered. It means respecting yourself enough to have standards that prevent old patterns from creeping back in. Establishing and maintaining boundaries invites your partner to respect you and promotes a relationship based on equality rather than control or neediness. Healthy mutuality also means encouraging and supporting each other's personal growth—not losing sight of who you are as a unique individual in the process.

Creating conscious connections also involves active listening and presence. It's not enough to simply hear words; you have to tune into the emotions, intentions, and unspoken cues behind them. This level of attentiveness builds intimacy and trust, showing your partner that they matter beyond surface-level exchanges. When both people feel truly listened to, it breaks down walls of defensiveness and fosters deeper understanding.

One practical way to develop conscious and mutual connections is by setting clear expectations early on. This doesn't mean listing demands but rather conversationally sharing what you value in a relationship and what you're willing to contribute. Open communication about needs and boundaries helps prevent misunderstandings, resentment, and codependent slipbacks. For example, if you need space to process emotions or time for self-care, expressing that clearly invites acceptance and respect instead of conflict.

It's also essential to become aware of your triggers and old patterns as you engage in new relationships. For many, subconscious fears or habits can sabotage what might otherwise be healthy connections. When you notice feelings of anxiety, clinginess, or withdrawal popping up, take a moment to reflect instead of reacting impulsively. Recognizing and responding to these internal cues is a skill that grows over time but is invaluable for maintaining conscious interaction.

Moreover, understanding interdependence helps distinguish truly mutual connections from relationships where emotional fusion is mistaken for closeness. Emotional fusion, common in codependent relationships, blurs individual boundaries and creates a co-dependent dynamic that eventually drains both people. Interdependent relationships, on the other hand, celebrate two autonomous individuals choosing connection without losing themselves.

One might ask, how do you know when a connection is truly mutual? A helpful indicator is whether both partners feel safe expressing discomfort or disagreement without fearing rejection. Mutual connections allow vulnerability but never at the cost of personal integrity or emotional well-being. You'll notice a natural rhythm of giving and receiving that feels nourishing—not exhausting.

Trust plays a huge role here, but building trust after codependency takes time. It requires showing up consistently, honoring commitments, and being reliable—not just for the other person but for yourself. You develop trust in the relationship by trusting your own judgment and refusing to ignore red flags. This self-trust shapes the entire dating process, guiding you toward connections that reflect your healing journey.

The conscious partner also checks in regularly with themselves, asking tough questions: Am I feeling respected? Does this relationship support my growth? Am I maintaining my boundaries? These reflections keep you grounded in your values and prevent slipping into old habits that might once have felt safe but now only lead to self-neglect.

Importantly, conscious and mutual connections often flourish from shared emotional responsibility. Rather than trying to "fix" your partner or take their emotional burdens onto yourself, each person owns their feelings and communicates them openly. This doesn't mean ignoring empathy or support; on the contrary, it means offering that support from a space of strength rather than obligation. Healthy relationships invite collaboration in managing feelings and navigating challenges together.

There's also beauty in nurturing each other's independence. Encouraging your partner's interests, friendships, and self-care routines fosters lifelong bonds that are resilient rather than codependent. When both people thrive individually, the relationship becomes a source of joy and strength—not a chain or safety net.

Of course, consciousness in connection isn't about perfection or having all the answers. It's about showing up with intention and willingness to learn, adapt, and grow alongside a partner. Mistakes will happen, and old insecurities might show up from time to time. What matters is practicing self-compassion and recommitting to boundaries and authentic communication after those moments.

In sum, dating after codependency invites you to create relationships that are grounded in awareness and equality—a stark contrast to past patterns where codependency ruled. This path encourages a new way of loving: one where you honor your emotions, set boundaries without guilt, and cherish reciprocal care. By doing so, you build connections that not only provide companionship but also foster emotional freedom and shared empowerment.

As you move forward, remember that creating conscious and mutual connections is a dynamic process that unfolds over time. Each interaction is an opportunity to deepen understanding, test boundaries, and celebrate authentic partnership. This journey doesn't just transform how you relate to others; it reshapes your whole relationship with yourself.

CHAPTER 14

Living Authentically in All Relationships

Embracing authenticity in every connection means showing up as your true self without masks or pretenses, which can feel both liberating and vulnerable at once. When you commit to living authentically, you set the tone for deeper, more meaningful interactions that honor your needs and values while respecting those of others. This isn't just about romantic partnerships; it extends to family, friends, coworkers, and social circles, where clarity and honesty foster trust and mutual respect. By grounding your relationships in genuine expression and mindfulness, you break free from the exhausting patterns of codependency and create space for resilient, balanced bonds that grow from transparency, not obligation or fear. Living authentically invites growth for everyone involved and encourages a cycle of connection rooted in freedom rather than control or people-pleasing.

Applying Interdependence Principles with Family and Friends

Living authentically in all relationships means extending the principles of interdependence beyond romantic partnerships into the realm of family and friendship. These relationships often carry deep emotional histories, long-standing patterns, and unspoken expectations, making the practice of healthy interdependence both challenging and profoundly rewarding. Unlike codependent patterns—where boundaries blur and one's sense of self becomes enmeshed in the other—it's about finding a balance where individuality and connection coexist harmoniously.

Family dynamics can be especially complex because of the shared history and emotional bonds that run deep. Old roles often resurface, like the caretaker, the peacemaker, or the scapegoat, which can sabotage authentic connection if left unchecked. Applying interdependence principles means recognizing these patterns without judgment and actively choosing to redefine how you show up. This shift starts with owning your emotional autonomy. You acknowledge your feelings, beliefs, and needs as valid and separate from others', even when those needs clash with established family expectations.

When interacting with family members, communication needs to be both honest and compassionate. Speaking your truth doesn't mean confrontation or conflict—it means sharing your perspective clearly while remaining open to theirs. This practice fosters mutual respect and creates space where everyone can express their individuality. Over time, these conversations can dismantle unhealthy cycles of control or emotional fusion that often characterize strained family relationships.

Friendships, too, benefit enormously from embracing interdependence. Friendships based on mutual support rather than obligation build resilience. Instead of trying to fix one another or over-involving yourselves in each other's problems, friends practicing interdependence offer presence and encouragement while respecting personal boundaries. This respect preserves each individual's autonomy, allowing both parties to grow independently while staying emotionally connected.

One critical aspect of applying interdependence with family and friends is managing expectations realistically. It's common to expect that family members or long-term friends will respond or behave in specific ways because of shared history or unspoken agreements. However, holding onto rigid expectations often leads to disappointment and resentment. Shifting toward interdependence invites flexibility—accepting that others have their own journeys and boundaries—and responding with curiosity rather than frustration when things don't go as hoped.

This shift often requires putting new skills into practice. Setting and maintaining boundaries is key. For example, choosing when to engage in difficult conversations and knowing when to step back to preserve your emotional well-being helps prevent old patterns from re-emerging. It's also essential to honor your limits around emotional labor—recognizing that supporting others isn't your sole responsibility, and it's okay to say no without guilt. This frees you to show up fully when you do choose to engage.

Equally important is learning to receive support graciously. Many who have struggled with codependency get used to being the "giver" and feel uncomfortable asking for help themselves. With family and friends, authentic interdependence is not one-sided. It's a dance back and forth of giving and receiving. Allowing yourself to be vulnerable and accept others' kindness strengthens bonds and reduces the pressure that comes with carrying everything alone.

It can also be helpful to gently challenge unhealthy relational habits in these connections without trying to change the other person. When old dynamics arise—like over-dependence or control attempts—naming them calmly and redirecting the interaction toward mutual respect nourishes healthier exchanges. Remember, your growth doesn't depend on changing others but on how you choose to respond. Modeling interdependence through your actions can slowly encourage those around you to do the same.

Family and friendships also invite opportunities for expressing appreciation and gratitude, which serve as vital emotional nutrients. Acknowledging the positive qualities of others keeps relationships balanced and affirming. When you express sincere appreciation, it fosters goodwill and deepens connection. This practice is especially powerful in relationships previously shadowed by codependency, as it shifts the focus away from dysfunction and toward genuine value.

Another cornerstone of healthy interdependence with family and friends is patience. Long-standing patterns and emotional wounds don't transform overnight. Accepting that change is a gradual process allows you to extend kindness to both yourself and others as you navigate new ways of relating. Sometimes, stepping back and prioritizing self-care might be necessary to maintain your boundaries and sanity while the relationship evolves.

In many cases, applying these principles means choosing to surround yourself with individuals who respect your growth and support your journey toward authenticity. Family relationships can be deeply meaningful, but sometimes, certain ties must be re-evaluated or even distanced if they consistently undermine your well-being. Friends, on the other hand, can be chosen and cultivated with intention. Investing time in relationships that honor your autonomy and emotional health sustains the foundation of interdependence.

It's important to remember that interdependence doesn't eliminate differences or disagreements. Instead, it equips you to engage with them in ways that promote understanding rather than withdrawal or conflict. Viewing challenges as opportunities for mutual learning aligns with living authentically, encouraging connections where each person feels seen and empowered.

Ultimately, applying interdependence principles with family and friends reshapes how you experience closeness. It empowers you to participate authentically, without sacrificing your identity or emotional well-being. As your relationships evolve through this lens, you'll find they become not only sources of comfort and joy but also reflections of your own continuing growth and resilience. Living authentically means carrying this mindset across all your interactions—whether rooted in biology or choice—and nurturing relationships where everyone can be their fullest selves.

Navigating Professional and Social Relationships Mindfully

When it comes to living authentically, extending that principle beyond intimate partnerships into professional and social spheres is crucial. It's common to feel pressure in these environments to conform, people-please, or avoid conflict, especially if codependency patterns have influenced your earlier relationships. But mindful navigation of these spaces means recognizing that authenticity doesn't just belong in your personal life—it's a practice that bolsters resilience, clarity, and connection everywhere.

One of the first steps is understanding that professional and social relationships operate within unique dynamics. Unlike romantic relationships, these connections often require a different balance between self-expression and diplomacy. At work, for example, maintaining professionalism sometimes feels like you need to mute parts of yourself. Still, this doesn't mean you have to sacrifice your values or boundaries to fit in or be accepted. The skill lies in being genuine without oversharing or compromising your emotional well-being.

When you approach your interactions mindfully, you begin to notice the subtle signs of codependent tendencies creeping in: excessive people-pleasing to gain approval, avoiding tough conversations to keep the peace, or feeling responsible for others' emotions. These patterns can quickly erode your authenticity and leave you drained. Instead, practicing mindfulness lets you catch these urges early and pause before reacting. It opens space to respond thoughtfully, maintaining both your integrity and your relationship's health.

The workplace often demands collaboration and teamwork, which means listening and expressing yourself effectively while respecting others' contributions. Cultivating emotional intelligence is vital here. Emotional intelligence isn't about suppressing your feelings but rather recognizing and managing them in ways that serve the situation and relationship. When you're emotionally attuned, you're better equipped to set boundaries clearly, communicate needs assertively, and navigate conflicts without falling into old codependency traps like guilt or fear of rejection.

Mindful navigation isn't just about avoiding pitfalls. It also means building meaningful connections based on respect and mutual understanding. In social settings, this might look like creating friendships where both parties feel comfortable being themselves without pressure to perform or please consistently. It's about choosing relationships that honor your values and offer reciprocal support rather than one-sided emotional labor.

Sometimes, breaking free of unhealthy patterns in these areas requires relearning how relationships actually work. For many, the belief that being liked or accepted requires perfect behavior is so ingrained it feels like truth. Mindfulness helps unravel this by inviting curiosity and nonjudgmental awareness. When you notice yourself slipping into "yes" mode or hiding feelings to avoid conflict, you can gently explore what's driving that response. Are you afraid of being rejected? Trying to keep control? Wanting to be "good enough"? Naming these fears empowers you to move beyond them.

Another important aspect is recognizing that your worth isn't tied to your productivity or social popularity. In professional circles, it's easy to conflate success with the ability to please others or maintain a flawless image. Mindfulness teaches you to anchor your self-esteem in who you are internally, not how others perceive or value you. This shift creates a foundation for authenticity that protects against burnout and emotional exhaustion.

Practically speaking, navigating professional relationships mindfully might involve setting clear boundaries around your time and energy. Saying "no" to extra projects that don't align with your goals or declining social invitations you're not up for are acts of self-respect. These choices can feel uncomfortable at first, especially if you're used to prioritizing others' needs, but each small step strengthens your autonomy. Over time, colleagues and social contacts will come to respect this consistency, even if it surprises them initially.

Conflict often arises in the workplace and social settings, and approaching it mindfully can make all the difference. Rather than avoiding discomfort or reacting impulsively, mindfulness invites you to hold space for dialogue while maintaining your boundaries. You don't have to win every argument or be the peacekeeper at all costs. Instead, focus on expressing your perspective honestly and listening openly, without internalizing others' criticisms or taking disagreements personally.

Social media and digital communication add another layer to professional and social navigation. The temptation to curate an idealized version of yourself is strong, yet this often creates disconnect rather than connection. Mindful engagement online means being intentional about how much you share, choosing when to engage or disengage, and staying true to your values. It also means recognizing when digital interactions drain your emotional energy and taking breaks when needed.

Finding balance in professional and social circles also requires a commitment to self-care and reflection. Regularly checking in with yourself about how interactions are affecting you helps you maintain alignment with your authentic self. Sometimes that means adjusting your environment—seeking new social groups, mentors, or professional teams that encourage growth and respect your evolving boundaries. Other times, it's about deepening the quality of existing relationships by bringing more honesty and vulnerability to the table.

It's worth acknowledging that living authentically in public spheres isn't about perfection or having all the answers. There will be moments of discomfort, missteps, and learning curves. Mindfulness is your ally in these moments, helping you observe what's happening without harsh judgment or retreat into old survival habits. Each challenge is an opportunity to practice resilience and reinforce your commitment to genuine connection.

Lastly, approaching these relationships mindfully invites you to consider your impact on others as well. Interdependence isn't one-sided—it's about mutual caretaking where both you and those around you thrive. This means showing empathy without enabling, offering support while encouraging autonomy, and celebrating others' successes without losing sight of your own journey.

In sum, navigating professional and social relationships mindfully is about bringing your whole self into every interaction with awareness, intention, and courage. It's learning to say yes and no in ways that preserve your integrity. It's about listening and speaking in balanced ways that deepen connection rather than blur boundaries. Most importantly, it's recognizing that your authenticity is your greatest asset—not just in love but in every relationship you choose to invest in.

CHAPTER 15

Your Relationship With Yourself

Building a healthy, lasting relationship with yourself is the foundation for any balanced connection you'll create with others, and it starts by recognizing your own worth outside of external validation or past patterns of codependency. When you treat yourself as your own safe space—offering kindness, patience, and honest reflection—you begin to cultivate the emotional independence that allows you to show up fully in relationships without losing yourself. This means developing daily habits that nurture your inner strength, like checking in with your feelings, honoring your needs without guilt, and embracing imperfections as part of your growth journey.

This chapter invites you to shift the focus inward and see yourself not just as someone deserving love from others, but as someone capable of loving, trusting, and relying on yourself with confidence and compassion.

Daily Habits for Self-Love and Independence

Building a healthy relationship with yourself is a continuous journey, one best supported by daily habits that nurture self-love and cultivate independence. These habits don't need to be grand or complicated; in fact, small consistent actions hold immense power over time. When you commit to daily practices that reinforce your worth and autonomy, you gradually replace old patterns of dependency with confidence and resilience.

It's easy to overlook the importance of the everyday. You might think that healing and growth require big leaps, but often it's the steady momentum built through routine habits that lifts us out of codependent cycles. Start by carving out moments during your day where you focus solely on yourself—not as an afterthought, but as a priority. This could be as simple as five minutes spent checking in with your emotions or expressing gratitude for your efforts. By doing this, you're signaling to yourself that your needs matter, that you are worthy of care and attention. Over time, this reinforces your self-esteem in subtle yet profound ways.

Self-love thrives on kindness, and habitual kindness towards yourself builds an internal sense of safety. Instead of falling into harsh self-criticism or comparison, try adopting a gentle tone in your inner dialogue. When you catch yourself thinking negatively, pause and challenge those thoughts. Ask: "Would I say this to a good friend?" If the answer is no, consider reframing your thoughts with encouragement or compassion. The goal isn't to be unrealistically positive, but to treat yourself with the same respect and care you would offer someone you love.

Another essential daily habit for fostering independence is learning to be comfortable with your own company. In codependent relationships, loneliness often feels unbearable, tempting you to seek constant validation or avoid being alone at almost any cost. Reclaiming your own space with ease takes practice. Schedule regular periods where you intentionally spend time by yourself doing activities that bring you joy or peace—whether that's reading, taking a walk, cooking a meal, or simply sitting quietly. These moments reconnect you with your preferences, interests, and rhythms without needing input or approval from others.

Alongside solitude, cultivating mindfulness is a cornerstone habit that deepens your emotional awareness and presence. Mindfulness isn't about escaping your feelings but learning to observe them without judgment. When practiced daily, maybe through meditation, deep breathing, or mindful movement, it trains your brain to respond rather than react. This shift is crucial for breaking free from codependency, where emotions often trigger impulsive behaviors or people-pleasing responses. Instead, mindfulness strengthens your ability to recognize what you truly want or need in any given moment.

The way you care for your body directly influences how you feel about yourself. Incorporating physical self-care into your routine is more than just about health—it's an act of respect toward your being. Whether it's regular exercise, nourishing meals, or adequate sleep, these habits remind you that your body deserves time and attention. Paying attention to bodily needs reconnects you to yourself in ways the mind alone cannot achieve. When you feel physically strong and rested, your emotional capacity to stand on your own two feet grows.

Journaling a few minutes each day can be a transformational tool as well. Writing down your thoughts, emotions, and progress encourages self-reflection and self-expression. It provides a safe space to explore your internal world without censorship or fear. Over time, journaling reveals patterns, celebrates victories, and helps untangle complicated feelings. You don't need a perfect diary or lengthy entries—simply putting pen to paper can help you become more attuned to your inner voice and build trust in yourself.

Developing a habit of setting small, realistic goals every day further strengthens independence. These goals don't have to be monumental; they could be as simple as saying "no" once when you usually say "yes" out of guilt or practicing assertive communication in a minor interaction. Each successful step away from old dependencies empowers you to reclaim control over your choices and boundaries. It's a way to prove to yourself consistently that living on your own terms is not only possible but satisfying.

Another powerful daily habit involves celebrating your progress, no matter how small. Growth often feels slow or invisible, especially when healing wounds from codependent patterns. Taking a moment to acknowledge your effort and resilience encourages motivation to keep moving forward. You might end the day by mentally listing three things you did well or aspects of yourself you appreciate. These accumulated affirmations gradually reshape your self-image from one that relies on external approval to one that is internally grounded.

Learning to ask for help when you need it is sometimes overlooked in discussions about independence, but it's actually a vital habit that fosters healthy autonomy. It can feel counterintuitive to reach out, especially if previous experiences taught you to be overly self-reliant or hesitant to expose vulnerability. Practicing to identify when you need support and then consciously seeking it from trusted sources—whether a friend, therapist, or support group—builds interdependence rather than dependence. It teaches you that true strength includes knowing your limits and honoring them.

Gratitude is another simple yet profound habit to weave into your everyday life. Instead of focusing on what's missing or what others might be doing wrong, regularly reminding yourself of what you have and what you bring to the table reorients your mindset. Gratitude shifts the focus inward, highlighting your abundance and qualities you've cultivated regardless of relationship dynamics. This shift is foundational in fostering a balanced internal world where self-sufficiency and appreciation coexist.

While cultivating independence, recognize the importance of flexibility within your habits. Life is unpredictable, and rigid routines can sometimes lead to frustration or feelings of failure. Instead, allow room for adjustment and self-compassion when your day doesn't go as planned. Remember, the goal of these daily habits isn't perfection—they're tools to help you build a stronger, kinder relationship with yourself. Consistently returning to your intentions, even after setbacks, keeps your progress steady and sustainable.

Finally, recognize that daily habits for self-love and independence are not about isolating yourself from others but building a firm foundation within so you can engage with the world from a place of authenticity and strength. When your sense of self is clear and nurtured, your relationships naturally become more balanced, interdependent, and enriching. You stop seeking validation to fill gaps and instead bring whole, confident presence into your connections.

Incorporating these habits into your daily life can feel challenging at first, especially if you're emerging from patterns of codependency. But every act of self-care and assertion, no matter how small, is a declaration of your worth and freedom. Over time, these simple yet powerful habits weave a fabric of self-love and autonomy that supports your growth and happiness far beyond what you might have imagined possible.

Becoming Your Own Safe Space and Source of Strength

Learning to become your own safe space is one of the most transformative steps you can take on the path to emotional independence and healthy interdependent relationships. When you rely on yourself to provide comfort, reassurance, and strength, you're no longer at the mercy of others' moods, reactions, or approval. This shift doesn't happen overnight. It takes intention, patience, and a willingness to face uncomfortable truths. But the reward is profound: a grounded sense of safety that stays steady no matter what storms may come your way.

At its core, becoming your own safe space means developing an internal refuge you can turn to in moments of stress, doubt, or fear. Picture this: instead of scrambling for external validation or support every time things get tough, you pause and connect inwardly, offering yourself kindness and understanding. This is radically different from the old codependent scripts that taught you to outsource your emotional well-being to others, often sacrificing your needs in the process. Your inner refuge becomes a sanctuary where you honor your feelings without judgment and remind yourself that you are enough—as you are.

Building this safe space starts with developing self-awareness and self-compassion, both of which are essential tools in rewriting your emotional narrative. The more you practice turning toward yourself with curiosity and care during difficult moments, the less intimidating those moments become. You may find that you no longer fear feeling vulnerable or overwhelmed because you know you have what it takes to navigate through those feelings. That steady internal presence becomes a source of strength—a kind of emotional resilience that empowers you to show up authentically in relationships without losing yourself.

Many people struggle with the idea of self-reliance because they've mistaken independence for isolation. But becoming your own safe space isn't about shutting others out or going it alone. It's about nurturing a solid foundation within yourself that allows you to enter relationships as a whole, balanced person—not someone dependent on constant reassurance or rescue. There's a subtle but powerful difference between needing others to feel safe and choosing to create safety within yourself while still engaging meaningfully with those you love.

One of the first practical moves toward becoming your own sanctuary is learning how to calm your inner critic and soothe emotional distress on your own terms. This might look like developing calming rituals: taking mindful breaths, journaling about your feelings, or talking kindly to yourself as you would to a close friend. The goal isn't to erase difficult feelings but to hold space for them without spiraling. When you build these skills, you start to break free from reactive patterns and replace them with responsive choices aligned with your well-being.

It can help to think of your inner safe space as a muscle that needs consistent attention and training. Maybe sometimes it feels strong, steady, and inviting—and other times it feels fragile or neglected. That's normal. The key is to keep showing up for yourself, especially in moments when you want to look outward for relief. Over time, the habit of self-soothing strengthens your emotional core, giving you more freedom to engage fully in relationships without losing your center.

Part of this journey often involves rewriting the messages you received growing up—that you're only valuable if you meet others' expectations or that your emotions are too much to carry alone. It takes courage to challenge those beliefs and to say, "I am worthy of kindness and support, starting with myself." This kind of internal validation is a powerful shield against falling back into patterns of codependency that kept you stuck in unhealthy cycles. By becoming your own source of strength, you reclaim the power to regulate your emotions in ways that honor your experience and keep you grounded.

Another important aspect is cultivating a relationship with yourself that includes celebration and gentle accountability. It's about recognizing your small victories and forgiving your setbacks. Sometimes you will feel vulnerable or overwhelmed, and that's okay. It doesn't mean you've lost your safe space; it means you're human. The difference is that instead of spiraling into self-criticism or seeking external validation to soothe those moments, you turn inward with a compassionate presence. This internal refuge can hold all parts of you—the brave and the scared, the confident and the uncertain—without needing to fix or change anything immediately.

To make this more tangible, consider creating rituals or practices that remind you of your safe space throughout the day. This could be as simple as setting an intention each morning, repeating affirming mantras, or visualizing a place where you feel completely at ease. These little anchors reconnect you to your inner strength and help you build a habit of self-soothing before external stresses can take over. Eventually, when challenges arise, you already have a resilient core to support you.

It's also essential to acknowledge that this work isn't about perfection. You won't always feel strong or safe, and sometimes you'll slip back into old reliance patterns. What matters is that you keep returning to yourself with patience and gentleness. Becoming your own safe space is an ongoing practice, not a final destination, and treating it as such relieves a lot of unnecessary pressure. With each step you take toward emotional independence, you're proving to yourself that you have everything you need to thrive inside.

When you embrace this internal sanctuary, relationships with others start to shift in profound ways. You show up more fully, communicate your needs clearly, and form connections that are based on mutual respect and genuine closeness rather than fear or dependence. This freedom allows you to engage with vulnerability without losing your boundaries or sense of self. Over time, your partnerships, friendships, and family relationships can become nourished by the strength you carry within, rather than weakened by the emptiness of unmet expectations.

In the end, becoming your own safe space and source of strength is about reclaiming your emotional autonomy. It's about realizing that the ground you stand on doesn't have to shake because others falter. You build a home within yourself—a refuge of compassion, courage, and unwavering support that becomes the foundation for all your relationships. This inner home is where you start, return, and grow, no matter the challenges life or love may bring your way.

Remember, the journey toward becoming your own safe space might feel like a winding road, but every step forward strengthens your emotional resilience and deepens your capacity for true interdependence. Keep nurturing this space with love, intention, and grace—because you deserve the safety and strength that come from within.

CHAPTER 16

REBUILDING TRUST IN YOURSELF AND OTHERS

After breaking free from unhealthy relationship patterns, rebuilding trust in yourself and others can feel like starting from scratch, but it's an essential step toward creating balanced, interdependent connections. Trust doesn't just appear overnight—it grows steadily through consistent actions, honest communication, and self-compassion. Learning to rely on your own judgment and honoring your needs cultivates inner confidence, which naturally spills over into how you engage with others. While vulnerability can feel risky at first, showing up authentically and setting clear boundaries invites others to respond with respect and reliability. This process requires patience and forgiveness, recognizing that setbacks may happen, but each moment of choosing trust moves you closer to emotionally fulfilling relationships that support your freedom and growth.

Understanding Trust After Codependency

Rebuilding trust after living through codependency isn't about flipping a switch or deciding one day to trust instantly. It's a gradual journey—one that requires patience, self-compassion, and willingness to face uncomfortable truths. When you've repeatedly put others' needs above your own, or felt your sense of safety tied directly to someone else's approval or presence, trust becomes complicated. You might find yourself questioning your own judgment or doubting whether people can truly be reliable. This is a natural response to the emotional lessons codependency has taught you, but it doesn't define your future relationships.

Codependency often distorts how trust develops and functions in our lives. Instead of trust growing from mutual respect and reliability, it's tangled with fear of abandonment, approval-seeking, and an overwhelming need to control relationships in order to feel safe. When your emotional well-being has been so closely linked to others' actions or moods, it's easy to confuse codependent behavior for trust. The catch is that this kind of "trust" is fragile and conditional; it only holds up when your partner behaves exactly as expected. That's a precarious place to be, fundamentally unstable and exhausting.

Reassessing what trust means for you personally is the first step to healthy healing. Real trust doesn't shy away from vulnerability; it embraces it as part of connection rather than fearing exposure. It starts with learning to trust yourself—your instincts, your feelings, your needs—and understanding that you are worthy of reliability and respect. This rebuilding doesn't mean ignoring past hurts or pretending they didn't happen. Instead, it's about creating a new foundation, one that acknowledges those wounds but isn't governed by them.

After codependency, your inner voice might send you mixed signals. You might feel torn between wanting to believe in others and fearing that trust will only lead to disappointment—because it has before. These conflicting feelings are expected. The goal isn't to eliminate all fear but to work through it bit by bit, strengthening your emotional muscles so fear doesn't control your choices. Practicing this internal balancing act takes time and repeated effort, but each step forwards makes trust feel more attainable and authentic.

One common struggle after codependency is the tendency to rush back into familiar patterns, especially when rebuilding relationships. The discomfort of uncertainty can push you to seek immediate reassurance or prove loyalty prematurely, which ironically undermines the very trust you're trying to nurture. Learning to sit with that discomfort—to be patient and set healthy boundaries around the pace of connection—is crucial. Trust flourishes when it's allowed to unfold naturally, rather than being forced or manipulated out of insecurity.

It's also essential to acknowledge how trust intersects with self-awareness in this process. Recognizing your own triggers, patterns, and emotional responses helps you understand why certain people or situations challenge your ability to trust. When you see these patterns clearly, you gain the power to interrupt them before falling back into old habits. Developing this kind of emotional insight is fundamental to rebuilding trust because it creates space for conscious choice rather than automatic reaction.

Rebuilding trust doesn't happen in isolation. While a lot of work happens within yourself—reconnecting with your worth, cultivating self-validation—it also involves real interplay with others. This means learning to observe behaviors and intentions without jumping to conclusions or letting old fears dictate how you interpret actions. Healthy trust is based on consistent patterns over time. It's about reliability and openness from both sides, not one-off promises or idealized hopes.

Another layer worth exploring is the difference between trusting others and depending on them. Codependency often blurs these lines, making it tough to tell when trust is genuine or when it's a mask for unhealthy dependence. True trust respects boundaries and autonomy; it's flexible, not rigid. When you rebuild trust after codependency, you're also learning to dismantle the belief that your emotional survival depends solely on what others give you. This shift might feel unsettling, but it's liberating. It allows relationships to thrive on mutual support rather than emotional suffocation.

Forgiveness plays a subtle but critical role in restoring trust as well. Not forgiveness in the sense of diminished self-protection or excusing harmful behaviors, but forgiveness as a personal release from carrying bitterness. When you let go of resentment and blame, you make room for clearer, less reactive perceptions of yourself and others. This mental decluttering helps build a fresh emotional landscape where trust can grow more naturally.

In the aftermath of codependency, it's also helpful to redefine what "being trustworthy" means for you—not just in others but in yourself. This includes honoring your commitments, speaking your truth with compassion, and following through on your promises. When you learn to be a person you can trust, it sets a powerful precedent for how you expect others to treat you. Trust begins as a relationship you cultivate inwardly before it can flourish outwardly.

Understanding trust after codependency requires patience with the back-and-forth nature of healing. You might experience moments of hope followed by setbacks. This is part of the process, not a failure. Each time you choose to lean into trust despite the discomfort, you build resilience. You prove to yourself that you can hold your ground emotionally without losing your sense of safety.

It's important to keep in mind that no one else can give you trust—it's something you generate within and then allow in from relationships. This internal generation of trust is what breaks the cycle of codependency, where trust was often projected outward in unhealthy ways. You reclaim your power and redefine the rules of connection according to your authentic worth and value. The payoff is relationships that honor your needs while nurturing genuine closeness.

Lastly, trust after codependency isn't about perfection. No one can guarantee they will never disappoint or make mistakes. What matters is the overall pattern of respect, honesty, and accountability. This creates a safe enough environment for trust to flourish naturally. Rebuilding trust is walking toward connection with both courage and caution, ready to embrace growth while honoring your boundaries.

Steps to Cultivate Trust in New Relationships

Building trust in new relationships often feels like navigating a winding path—sometimes smooth, sometimes full of unexpected obstacles. After experiencing codependent dynamics, it's understandable to approach fresh connections with caution, or even skepticism. But trust isn't something that magically appears overnight; it's a process that requires patience, intentionality, and self-awareness. The key is to focus on small, consistent actions that gradually create a foundation where trust can grow both ways.

First, it's important to recognize that rebuilding trust starts with yourself. If you've been hurt or let down before, you might carry fears or doubts that cloud your ability to believe in new people. Before opening up fully, spend time grounding yourself in your own values and boundaries. When you know what you need and what you won't accept, it's easier to gauge if the other person aligns with those standards. This self-knowledge grounds your trust in reality rather than wishful thinking.

Next, transparency plays a huge role in cultivating trust. Being honest about who you are, what you want, and where you're coming from sets the tone for openness. This doesn't mean rushing to reveal your deepest secrets right away, but rather sharing your feelings and thoughts clearly and authentically. How the other person responds to that honesty is telling. Trust blossoms when both people allow vulnerability in manageable doses and demonstrate respect for each other's pace.

Consistent behavior speaks louder than words, especially in early days. People can say anything they want, but trust builds when actions reliably follow through on promises. If someone repeatedly cancels plans or overlooks what matters to you, those little breaches start to erode confidence. On the flip side, a partner who shows up when they say they will, listens attentively, and remembers your preferences proves that they value and respect you. Watching these small, concrete actions over time gives you a clear picture of whether trust is warranted.

Developing trust also involves setting and respecting boundaries. Boundaries aren't walls designed to keep people out; they're guidelines that protect your emotional space and clarify what feels safe. Early in a relationship, communicating your boundaries—whether about time, communication frequency, or personal topics—lays a blueprint for mutual respect. Observing how someone reacts to your limits reveals much about their character. Will they honor your needs without judgment, or pressure you to bend? Trust grows when boundaries are accepted as natural and necessary.

Another critical step is slowing down the pace of the relationship. It's tempting after painful experiences to either rush into connection or hold too tightly, but neither serves trust well. Allowing the relationship to unfold at a natural tempo creates room for getting to know the person beyond surface impressions. Taking time to observe how they interact with others, how they handle stress, and how consistent they are helps to confirm or reset your expectations. Trust builds when patience replaces urgency, and curiosity replaces fear.

Listening carefully is a powerful trust-building tool often underestimated in the excitement of new attraction. Practicing active listening means fully engaging with what the other person shares without immediately planning your response or interpreting their words through past wounds. This kind of listening fosters real understanding and signals that you're present and invested. When both people feel heard and validated, it naturally deepens trust because it creates emotional safety.

Being willing to accept imperfections—both yours and theirs—is another key part of cultivating trust. No one is flawless, and expecting perfection only sets the relationship up for disappointment. Recognizing that mistakes or missteps are part of learning to connect allows you to approach challenges with compassion and flexibility. Trust grows when both partners feel safe to be themselves, with all their quirks and flaws, without fear of immediate rejection.

It's also helpful to remain mindful of your internal signals as you engage with a new person. Pay close attention to your gut feelings and emotional responses. If something feels off, it's worth pausing to reflect rather than brushing it away in the name of hope or desperation. Conversely, moments of ease, laughter, and shared values are indicators to nurture. Trust deepens when you tune in, honor your instincts, and don't ignore red flags or moments of joy.

Particularly for those healing from codependency, cultivating patience with yourself through this journey is vital. You might find old patterns creeping back—people-pleasing, fear of abandonment, or over-giving. When these arise, it's okay to slow down or seek support rather than forcing connection. Trusting yourself to make healthy choices in relationships is just as important as trusting the other person. When you strengthen that inner trust, it becomes a compass guiding you toward greater emotional safety.

Transparency about your past experiences can also foster understanding in new relationships. You don't have to share everything right away, but gently expressing that you're learning to rebuild trust helps set realistic expectations. It invites empathy and allows room for your partner to support your growth instead of unintentionally triggering defense mechanisms. Building trust becomes a shared process rather than a one-sided expectation.

Integrating small rituals or consistent check-ins can provide practical support to trust-building. Whether it's a weekly conversation about how the relationship is feeling or simply confirming plans ahead of time, these steady interactions reinforce reliability. They carve out intentional space to express appreciation, discuss concerns, and celebrate progress together. Over time, these habits weave trust into the very fabric of the connection.

Lastly, remember that cultivating trust is cyclical and dynamic. It's perfectly normal to encounter setbacks or moments of doubt. How these are handled often matters more than the fact they occurred. Couples and friends who navigate mistakes with forgiveness, accountability, and renewed commitment tend to deepen trust rather than fracture it. Embracing trust as an ongoing, evolving part of your relationships empowers you to build connections that are truly resilient and nourishing.

Trust in new relationships isn't about perfect certainty, but about cultivating a safe, honest, and respectful environment where both people can grow. By grounding yourself in self-awareness, communicating transparently, honoring boundaries, and moving at a steady pace, you lay the foundation for trust to flourish. This deliberate approach frees you from repeating old patterns and moves you closer to the balanced, interdependent connections that bring lasting emotional fulfillment.

CHAPTER 17

Developing Emotional Resilience

Building emotional resilience means cultivating the ability to recover and grow stronger from the inevitable challenges that come with breaking free from unhealthy relationship patterns. It's about learning to sit with difficult feelings without letting them derail your progress or your sense of self-worth. Resilience gives you the strength to face setbacks with clarity and compassion, rather than falling into old cycles of dependence or self-doubt. This chapter invites you to deepen your inner resources, so when emotional storms arise, you remain grounded, steady, and able to respond in ways that honor your growth and your needs. Developing this toughness from within not only protects your heart but also empowers you to engage in interdependent relationships where both partners can thrive without losing themselves.

Practices to Strengthen Your Emotional Core

Building emotional resilience isn't something that happens overnight. It takes consistent, intentional effort to create a sturdy emotional core—a foundation strong enough to withstand life's inevitable challenges without losing your sense of balance. At its heart, strengthening your emotional core means developing a deep reservoir of inner strength that allows you to stay centered even when external circumstances feel chaotic or overwhelming. This stability is essential for anyone breaking free from unhealthy relationship patterns and striving toward interdependent connections that honor both partners' individuality.

One of the first steps in fortifying your emotional core is becoming comfortable with discomfort. Life throws curveballs, and emotional discomfort is part of the package. Instead of pushing away difficult feelings or trying to numb them, practice leaning into the sensations with curiosity and openness. This doesn't mean wallowing in pain or anxiety, but rather acknowledging the emotions without judgment. Over time, this leads to greater emotional tolerance, which is a key ingredient for resilience. When you stop fighting your emotions, they start to lose their hold over you, and your ability to respond thoughtfully rather than react impulsively improves.

Developing mindfulness is another powerhouse practice. Mindfulness invites you to focus on the present moment instead of spinning in past regrets or future worries. Simple mindfulness exercises—like paying attention to your breath, noticing physical sensations, or observing your thoughts as if they were clouds drifting by—can ground you when emotional turbulence threatens to take over. This grounding effect taps into your emotional core, reminding you that you have an internal space of calm to retreat to, no matter what's happening externally.

Alongside mindfulness, cultivating self-compassion plays a vital role. Many people caught in codependent patterns tend to be harsh critics of themselves. They replay mistakes endlessly or blame themselves for what's not working in relationships. But resilient emotional strength comes from a kinder inner voice. Practicing self-compassion means speaking to yourself as you would a close friend—with encouragement, patience, and understanding. When you treat yourself with gentleness, you create a safe emotional environment inside that supports healing and growth rather than shame and defeat.

Consistency matters quite a bit when building your emotional core. Resilience is like a muscle—the more you exercise it, the stronger it gets. This can take many forms, whether it's daily journaling to track emotions and identify patterns, regular physical activity to boost your mood and reduce stress, or dedicating time each day to engage in activities that bring you genuine joy and fulfillment. These elements all work together to keep your emotional well-being cultivated and nourished.

Another critical practice centers on learning to set healthy boundaries with yourself as much as with others. Emotional resilience involves protecting your energy and mental space. This means being honest about what feels manageable and what crosses your limits, even if it means disappointing others or reconsidering old habits of people-pleasing. Boundaries don't isolate you—they clarify what's safe and respectful, which ultimately strengthens your relationships and preserves your emotional balance.

Equally important is learning to regulate your emotions without suppressing them. This can feel tricky—expressing feelings openly while keeping them in check often seems contradictory. But emotional regulation is about recognizing your feelings, naming them, and deciding how to act in a way that serves your well-being. Simple techniques like taking a few deep breaths before responding, counting to ten, or stepping away from intense situations temporarily can help you avoid emotional overwhelm. Over time, these habits embed deeper emotional control that radiates from a well-developed core.

It's also valuable to cultivate a mindset of flexibility and adaptability. Life rarely follows a straight path, and relationships especially can throw unexpected challenges your way. When your emotional core is rigid, setbacks hit hard and can feel crushing. But developing mental flexibility means viewing obstacles as opportunities to learn rather than failures to avoid. This perspective keeps you moving forward rather than stuck, and it supports resilience by reminding you of your capacity to adjust and grow.

Building your emotional core also involves nurturing a strong connection with your values. When you're clear about what matters most to you—whether that's authenticity, respect, kindness, or independence—it anchors your decisions and reactions. This clarity creates a compass that guides you back to center, especially in moments of emotional turmoil or relational conflict. Staying aligned with your values boosts your confidence and strengthens your sense of self, making you less likely to lose your footing when challenged.

Another practice that reinforces emotional stamina is fostering supportive connections. While building inner strength is foundational, humans are inherently relational beings. Seeking and maintaining relationships that offer encouragement, honesty, and mutual respect refuel your resilience. Sometimes this means leaning on friends, family, or support groups who validate your experience and cheer your progress without enabling old patterns. These external networks become safe harbors where your emotional core can stretch and solidify with trusted reinforcement.

It's normal to encounter setbacks or moments of feeling fragile despite your efforts—strengthening your emotional core is a non-linear process. Practicing patience with yourself during these times is just as important as the active work you do. Recognize that healing is messy and that stumbling doesn't mean failure. Often, setbacks provide rich material for learning and growth if you harness them thoughtfully. Continuing to return to the core strengthening practices builds resilience over time and leads to sustainable balance.

Finally, embracing a spirit of gratitude supports emotional well-being. Gratitude doesn't erase difficulties, but it shifts your focus to what's working, what's whole, and what brings meaning in your life. Regularly reflecting on positive aspects—whether big or small—creates a mental environment where hope and joy can flourish. This positivity buffers the impact of stress and reinforces the sturdiness of your emotional core, making it easier to maintain interdependent, healthy relationships.

In summary, strengthening your emotional core involves a blend of internal practices—embracing discomfort, mindfulness, self-compassion, consistent self-care, emotional regulation, flexibility, and values clarity—along with cultivating supportive relationships and patience through setbacks. Each practice deepens your ability to stay grounded amid emotional storms, empowering you to build balanced, interdependent relationships that nourish your soul without sacrificing your autonomy. This work, while sometimes challenging, is a powerful investment in yourself and your future connections.

Handling Setbacks Without Losing Ground

Setbacks are inevitable on any journey toward emotional resilience, especially when you're breaking free from unhealthy relationship patterns. They can come in many forms—an unexpected argument, a relapse into old behaviors, or a moment of self-doubt that threatens to unravel the progress you've made. What separates those who thrive from those who falter is how they handle these moments without losing ground. This section is dedicated to equipping you with the mindset and strategies needed to face setbacks head-on, while continuing to build the emotional strength that sustains lasting change.

First, it's important to acknowledge that setbacks don't erase your progress. They are part of the learning process, not signs of failure. If you find yourself falling back into familiar but unhealthy patterns, recognize this as an opportunity to gain deeper insight into your triggers and vulnerabilities. Emotional resilience isn't about never stumbling; it's about being able to rise each time you fall, with more understanding and wisdom than before. Keeping this perspective prevents setbacks from becoming devastating and instead transforms them into springboards for further growth.

When a setback happens, the initial reaction often involves frustration, shame, or even self-criticism. These emotions, while natural, can quickly spiral if left unchecked. One effective way to stay grounded is to practice self-compassion—treating yourself with the same kindness you would offer a dear friend struggling through a similar experience. Remember, you're retraining your emotional patterns, a process that takes time and patience. Harsh judgment will only deepen emotional wounds and make it harder to regain footing.

At the heart of handling setbacks lies the ability to pause and reflect. This doesn't mean obsessing over what went wrong, but rather stepping back with a curious and nonjudgmental mindset to understand the circumstances. What triggered the relapse? Was it a specific emotional state, a particular interaction, or perhaps unmet needs? Journaling or talking safely to a trusted friend or counselor can help clarify these questions and release built-up tension. By understanding the roots of your setback, you turn moments of difficulty into valuable learning experiences.

The way you respond emotionally in the moment of a setback is critical. Practicing emotional regulation techniques learned earlier, such as mindful breathing, grounding exercises, or brief moments of meditation, can help you stay calm and avoid reactive behaviors that reinforce codependency or emotional fusion. The goal is to maintain control long enough to consider your next steps wisely, rather than acting impulsively out of fear or shame.

Another core aspect of managing setbacks is reconnecting with your values and goals. When doubts or frustration creep in, reminding yourself why you embarked on this path to emotional resilience can inspire renewed commitment. It's about looking past the temporary challenge to the bigger picture—your desire for healthy, interdependent relationships that allow freedom and authenticity. Keeping a written list of personal affirmations or intentions nearby can prove helpful in these moments of wavering confidence.

Support systems play a crucial role in helping you handle setbacks without losing ground. Whether it's a therapist, a support group, or trusted friends who understand your journey, leaning on others creates a buffer against isolation and discouragement. These allies can offer encouragement, perspective, and accountability when you feel stuck or tempted to revert to old patterns. Remember, asking for help is a sign of strength, not weakness, and shows your commitment to growth.

Sometimes setbacks come disguised as external relationship challenges—like a partner resisting change, a hurtful encounter with a family member, or a frustrating social dynamic. It's essential not to internalize these difficulties as personal failures but rather to view them as natural tests that help sharpen emotional resilience. Developing grace around imperfections—both yours and others'—frees you from the trap of expecting a flawless transformation overnight. Instead, it nurtures a steady determination to keep moving forward, even amid turbulence.

When setbacks feel overwhelming, breaking down what needs to happen next into small, manageable steps makes the process less intimidating. Instead of trying to fix everything at once, focus on achievable goals like practicing one boundary more mindfully or journaling reflections on one emotional trigger. Each small success strengthens your emotional core and builds momentum. This approach aligns with how change truly unfolds: gradual, often nonlinear progress that accumulates over time.

Learning to reframe setbacks can also be empowering. Instead of viewing them as regressions, think of them as necessary recalibrations—moments when you gain clarity about what works and what doesn't in your emotional landscape.

This viewpoint encourages curiosity and experimentation rather than defeat. Over time, as you accumulate experiences of bouncing back, your confidence in handling emotional challenges will deepen significantly.

In practical terms, setting up routines and rituals to safeguard your emotional well-being reduces vulnerability to setbacks. This might involve regular self-check-ins, relaxation practices, or scheduled connection with your support network. Having these proactive systems in place creates resilience by building a foundation that can withstand inevitable stresses without cracking. Remember, emotional resilience thrives on consistency as much as on self-awareness.

At the core of handling setbacks is the realization that emotional resilience is a skill, not an innate trait. It grows stronger each time you refuse to let a difficult moment define you. By embracing challenges as opportunities to practice patience, self-compassion, and intentional action, you gradually rewrite the inner narrative that once told you change was impossible. With persistence and grace, setbacks become markers of progress rather than obstacles.

Ultimately, the ability to handle setbacks without losing ground empowers you to create relationships based on true interdependence rather than dependency or control. When you recover from emotional turbulence with purpose and kindness toward yourself, you model strength and authenticity to those around you. This ripple effect nurtures healthier connections where both partners feel safe, valued, and free to grow individually and together.

The journey isn't always easy, and there will be times when you might want to give up. But remember that every resilient person has weathered storms just like you are facing now. What sets them apart is their refusal to allow setbacks to dictate their story. You can develop this grit, too, by practicing the strategies outlined here repeatedly and adapting them as you learn more about what serves you best.

By tracking your setbacks without judgment, leaning on your support network, reconnecting with your goals, and nurturing self-compassion, you create a powerful cycle of resilience. This cycle propels you toward relationships and a life defined not by old fears or codependency, but by healthy connection, confidence, and balance. Handling setbacks without losing ground isn't just about survival—it's about thriving on your own terms, step by step, day by day.

CHAPTER 18

Cultivating Mutual Respect in Partnerships

Mutual respect forms the backbone of any thriving partnership, creating a space where both individuals feel valued and understood without losing their sense of self. It's about recognizing each other's worth and approaching differences with an open heart, allowing for honest dialogue and growth instead of defensiveness or contempt. When respect is cultivated intentionally, it encourages partners to listen actively, honor boundaries, and respond thoughtfully even during conflicts, laying the groundwork for collaboration instead of confrontation. This kind of respect strengthens trust, supports emotional safety, and fosters a balanced dynamic where both people feel empowered to express their needs freely while honoring the other's perspective. Establishing these respectful habits may take effort, especially when old patterns try to creep back, but doing so transforms relationships from battlegrounds into partnerships of deep, lasting connection and shared resilience.

Recognizing and Expressing Respectful Behaviors

Respect is the cornerstone of any partnership that aims to thrive beyond mere coexistence. When individuals learn to recognize and express respectful behaviors, they lay a foundation for connection that is not only lasting but deeply nourishing. It's about more than just courteous words or polite actions; respect carries a profound intention to honor the other person's worth, boundaries, and individuality. For those emerging from unhealthy relationship patterns, understanding what respect genuinely looks like can dramatically transform how they relate to others and themselves.

At its core, respectful behavior means acknowledging your partner as a whole person—not someone to mold, control, or save. This recognition involves tuning into subtle dynamics that often go unnoticed: the tone of voice during a disagreement, the willingness to wait for someone to finish speaking, and the gentle refusal to dismiss feelings, even when they don't align with your own perspective. These everyday gestures communicate value and trust far louder than grand declarations or promises.

One of the challenges people face after years of codependency is that respect might feel unfamiliar or even threatening. When respect involves the creation of healthy boundaries, it can initially evoke fears of rejection or abandonment. These feelings are natural. It's important to remind yourself that respect means giving everyone—including yourself—the space to be authentic without coercion or pressure. It's an act of love, not a withdrawal of care.

Identifying respectful behaviors requires a shift in focus from controlling outcomes to honoring processes. For example, instead of reacting defensively when a partner disagrees, a respectful response involves actively listening and validating their experience, even if it differs from your own. This doesn't mean you have to agree, but it signals that their feelings matter and that your relationship is a safe place for honest expression. Over time, this builds emotional safety, which is crucial for breaking free from codependent cycles.

Expressing respect also means communicating with intention—choosing words that uplift rather than wound, asking questions instead of making assumptions, and genuinely checking in on how the other person feels. It's easy to slip into automatic patterns of criticism or sarcasm, especially in stressful moments. But practicing respectful language, even when it feels difficult, can slow down reactive patterns and open a space for healing dialogue.

Nonverbal cues are just as vital in conveying respect. Simple actions like maintaining eye contact, nodding in understanding, or offering a reassuring touch demonstrate attentiveness and care. They tell your partner that they are seen and valued beyond words. Consider how often disrespect shows itself not through what's said but how it's said—dismissive gestures, eye-rolling, or distracted behavior can all erode connection without a single harsh word spoken.

Respectful behavior thrives on consistency. Sporadic moments of kindness can't sustain a relationship if they're overshadowed by repeated patterns of neglect or disregard. Developing mutual respect means committing to daily small acts that affirm each person's dignity. It may be as simple as remembering an important detail shared weeks ago, or giving space when your partner needs quiet time to recharge. These seemingly minor actions accumulate, creating a climate where both individuals feel safe and honored.

For anyone building a partnership grounded in interdependence, respect means embracing vulnerability without judgment. Sharing your fears, hopes, and needs openly requires trust that your partner will respond with care, not contempt. Likewise, respecting your partner involves receiving their vulnerability with patience and kindness. This mutual exchange fosters intimacy without sacrificing independence.

Sometimes, respect manifests by allowing for disagreement without escalation. It's natural for two people to have differing views or preferences. The respectful approach accepts these differences as opportunities to learn rather than threats to connection. Instead of trying to "win" a conversation, cultivating respect means seeking understanding and finding middle ground or agreeing to disagree—without diminishing the other's experience.

Recognizing disrespect is just as crucial as acknowledging respect. Disrespect can be subtle or overt, but it always signals harm to the relational foundation. It might show up as interrupting, belittling, dismissing feelings, violating boundaries, or withholding communication. Becoming aware of these signs empowers individuals to address issues before resentment and pain grow too large to contain.

Learning to express respect also involves modeling self-respect. How you treat yourself often sets the tone for how others will treat you. Speaking kindly to yourself, honoring your boundaries, and practicing self-care signal to your partner that you value yourself. This discourages the old codependent habit of seeking validation at all costs. When you respect yourself, you naturally expect—and expect from others—the same standard in how you are treated.

In partnerships recovering from codependency, respect may feel unbalanced at times while new patterns are forming. Patience is key. Both partners are learning and adapting, often needing reminders or gentle corrections. The goal isn't perfection but steady growth toward mutual recognition that both people's feelings, thoughts, and needs matter equally.

Encouraging respectful behavior also means cultivating empathy. When you consciously try to view situations through your partner's lens, it opens pathways for compassion instead of judgment. This empathetic stance softens defenses and reduces conflict intensity, allowing space for constructive problem-solving. It also communicates respect at a deep emotional level—a recognition that your partner's inner world deserves your attention and care.

Respect creates a ripple effect in partnerships. When present, it enhances trust, nurtures emotional safety, and promotes authentic expression. Without it, relationships crumble into patterns of resentment, withdrawal, or co-dependence. Recognizing and expressing respectful behaviors is, therefore, an essential skill for anyone committed to forging balanced, interdependent bonds that promote healing and joy.

Transformation begins with awareness: noticing when respect is present and when it's missing. From there, intentional practice of respectful communication, consistent honoring of boundaries, and embracing empathy will build a relationship that stands resilient against old patterns and new challenges alike. Respect becomes not just an action but a way of being—a shared language that connects hearts while safeguarding individuality.

The journey toward mutual respect requires courage and commitment, especially when stepping away from familiar but unhealthy scripts. Still, the rewards are profound: relationships where both partners flourish, feel valued, and contribute freely. Recognizing and expressing respectful behaviors isn't a checklist; it's an ongoing dance—sometimes imperfect, always evolving—between two people choosing to honor one another every day.

Encouraging Respectful Conflict Resolution

Conflict is inevitable in any close relationship. When two people share their lives, differences in opinions, needs, and emotions naturally arise. However, what makes or breaks a partnership isn't the presence of conflict itself but how those conflicts are handled. Encouraging respectful conflict resolution is a cornerstone of cultivating mutual respect. It's about creating space where disagreements don't escalate into personal attacks or emotional shutdowns, but instead become opportunities for both partners to deepen understanding and strengthen their connection.

Many individuals who've experienced codependency or unhealthy relational patterns may fear conflict because it often felt unsafe or overwhelming in the past. They either avoided disagreements altogether or reacted in ways that sacrificed their own voice to keep the peace. This dynamic builds resentment and disconnect over time. Moving forward requires a shift—a conscious choice to approach disagreements with intention and care rather than avoidance or hostility.

One of the first steps in supporting respectful conflict resolution is recognizing the importance of staying present during difficult exchanges. It's easy to shut down, tune out, or explode with frustration when conversations get tough. Yet, commitment to mutual respect asks partners to lean into discomfort with curiosity rather than judgment. This doesn't mean tolerating disrespect or dismissing your own boundaries, but rather committing to listen fully and speak honestly without blaming or belittling.

Language plays a huge role here. The way feelings and concerns are expressed can either fan the flames or cool things down. For example, replacing "You always..." statements with "I feel..." messages changes the energy of the conversation. Instead of assigning fault, "I" statements invite the other person to understand your personal experience. This shift fosters empathy and reduces defensiveness, which lays a much gentler groundwork for resolution.

In many codependent relationships, conflict often triggers fears of abandonment or rejection. These fears can push partners to either become overly accommodating—to the point of self-sacrifice—or highly reactive, lashing out to protect themselves. Both responses hinder healthy resolution because they're rooted in survival rather than connection. It helps to acknowledge these fears openly, either internally or with your partner, and remind yourself that feeling anxious or vulnerable is part of growth. Mutual respect thrives when both partners feel safe enough to express their true feelings, even if those feelings are uncomfortable.

Another key element is pacing the discussion in ways that honor both individuals' emotional capacity. Sometimes, a conflict isn't resolved in a single conversation—and that's okay. Being respectful means knowing when to pause, take a breath, and revisit the topic later if emotions run too high. This willingness to step back prevents hurtful words and allows space for both people to collect their thoughts, reducing the risk of regret or regretful reactions.

Respectful conflict resolution also involves genuinely seeking to understand your partner's perspective, even when it contradicts your own. This doesn't mean agreement is necessary but rather acknowledgment. Validation of feelings—letting your partner know you hear them—is a powerful way to deescalate tension. This approach naturally fosters trust and opens pathways to collaborative problem-solving rather than competition or winning an argument.

Part of encouraging respectful conflict resolution is also about building shared skills and tools that promote non-violent communication. These skills might include active listening—where one partner repeats back what they heard to ensure clarity—using calming techniques like grounding breaths, or setting mutually agreed-upon check-in points during heated discussions. Couples who invest in these skills demonstrate through action their respect for each other's emotional experience and their commitment to preservation of the relationship itself.

It's important to remember, respect doesn't mean suppressing disagreement or sweeping issues under the rug. In fact, healthy relationships allow for honest, even challenging conversations without fear of losing one another. The goal isn't conflict avoidance but rather transforming disagreements into growth moments where both partners feel heard, seen, and valued for their authenticity.

For individuals breaking free from codependent cycles, fostering respectful conflict resolution may demand extra patience and self-compassion. Past patterns of emotional fusion or people-pleasing may have trained them to prioritize others' feelings at the expense of their own voice. Learning to assert needs clearly and calmly while maintaining openness to feedback can feel daunting but becomes a vital part of rebuilding self-worth and establishing healthier relational dynamics.

Encouragement also comes from recognizing small wins in everyday interactions. Celebrating moments where disagreements occurred without yelling, blaming, or withdrawal builds confidence and creates a positive feedback loop. It shows that conflict can coexist with respect and that both partners can grow through the process. Over time, this cultivates resilience—a vital attribute in interdependent relationships where both autonomy and togetherness are honored.

One common stumbling block is the tendency to equate respectful conflict resolution with perfection, which sets unrealistic expectations. Nobody manages conflicts flawlessly every time. Compassionate forgiveness—both of yourself and your partner—is part of the journey. What matters most is returning to respectful communication after setbacks, recommitting to growth instead of allowing frustration or hopelessness to erode progress.

Ultimately, encouraging respectful conflict resolution means creating an environment where both partners feel secure enough to express dissatisfaction, disappointment, or hurt without fear of retaliation or dismissal. It nurtures an emotional climate that prioritizes listening and understanding over winning or shutting down. This careful balance nurtures mutual respect, which in turn strengthens the foundation of interdependence.

When conflicts are addressed respectfully, relationships shift from battlegrounds into places of healing and connection. They become spaces where both partners acknowledge their flaws and vulnerabilities without shame or blame. This openness invites compassion and invites growth on an individual and shared level. Respectful conflict resolution is less about avoiding trouble and more about learning how to weather difficult moments with integrity and kindness.

For those seeking freedom from unhealthy patterns, this approach offers a roadmap to reclaim power within relationships without sacrificing compassion. It teaches that honoring oneself and honoring a partner are not opposing forces, but rather complementary steps towards lasting closeness and emotional fulfillment. When respect guides how conflict is resolved, the partnership evolves into a safe haven—a place where individuality and intimacy thrive side by side.

CHAPTER 19

NAVIGATING INTIMACY WITH CONFIDENCE

Finding the balance between showing vulnerability and maintaining your personal boundaries is key to building intimacy that feels safe and genuine. It's natural to want to connect deeply, but it takes courage to protect your sense of self while opening up to another person. Confidence in intimacy grows from trusting yourself to communicate honestly, honoring both your needs and your partner's, and recognizing that healthy closeness doesn't require losing your independence. When you embrace this balance, you create space for a relationship where both people can thrive—feeling seen, understood, and respected without sacrificing who they are.

This chapter guides you to step into that kind of connection with strength and grace, encouraging you to let intimacy be a source of confidence rather than fear.

Balancing Vulnerability and Personal Boundaries

Opening yourself up in a relationship feels risky. Vulnerability invites intimacy, deep connection, and understanding—but it also exposes parts of yourself that feel tender and sometimes unsafe. The challenge isn't about choosing vulnerability over boundaries or vice versa; instead, it's finding a rhythm where both can coexist harmoniously. For those working to break free from codependent cycles and foster interdependent relationships, this balance becomes essential. It's the foundation for connecting authentically without losing your sense of self.

It's important to recognize that vulnerability and boundaries aren't opposing forces; they actually serve and protect one another. Boundaries create the safe container in which vulnerability can be expressed without sacrificing personal well-being. Without boundaries, vulnerability might lead to overexposure—sharing too much, too soon, or with the wrong person—and that often triggers old patterns of codependency where self-worth becomes entangled with another's approval. On the other hand, boundaries that are too rigid can block intimacy entirely. They keep people at a distance and prevent the trust-building that's necessary for meaningful relationships.

Many people struggle with balancing these elements because they've learned to view vulnerability as weakness. If you come from a background where emotional expression was punished or dismissed, it's understandable to keep walls firmly in place. But vulnerability, when embraced thoughtfully, is a source of strength. It's the gateway to showing up as your authentic self and inviting your partner or loved ones to do the same.

At the heart of this balancing act lies self-awareness. You need to tune in continuously to how vulnerable you feel and recognize the signals when you're beginning to step over your boundaries—or conversely, when you're shutting down to protect yourself too much. This doesn't just mean setting limits around what topics you discuss or how much time you spend with someone. It's also about understanding and honoring your emotional limits. Sometimes, you might feel ready to share your fears, dreams, or past wounds in bits and pieces rather than all at once, and that's okay. Vulnerability doesn't have to be an all-or-nothing offering; it's a process.

Equally, boundaries aren't fixed rules etched in stone. They should be flexible enough to evolve as your relationship deepens and as you grow personally. When you first start opening up, your limits may be quite firm to safeguard your emotional energy. Over time, those boundaries can shift, allowing deeper layers of trust and intimacy to emerge without losing your autonomy. It's a dynamic, ongoing dance rather than a one-time decision.

One way to cultivate this balance is by practicing clear communication about your needs and limits. For example, if you feel overwhelmed by someone's emotional intensity, expressing that honestly can prevent you from becoming enmeshed in their struggles or draining your own resources. On the flip side, inviting your partner to share their vulnerabilities and showing acceptance without judgment creates a safe space where intimacy thrives. This mutual exchange, grounded in respect for each person's boundaries, builds emotional resilience and trust.

Some might worry that enforcing boundaries could be perceived as rejection or create distance. But boundaries, when explained compassionately, actually enhance closeness. They tell the other person that you respect and value yourself, which encourages them to do the same. When people see you honoring your limits, it often motivates them to reflect on their own needs too, fostering healthier mutual respect. This can break the old codependent scripts where boundaries were blurred or ignored in an attempt to keep the relationship intact.

It also helps to redefine what vulnerability means in this context. Vulnerability isn't just about sharing your fears or struggles; it's also about revealing your values, hopes, and boundaries. It's inviting others into your world with honesty about what feels nourishing and what doesn't. For instance, saying "I need some time alone to recharge after social events" is a form of vulnerability paired with a boundary. It expresses self-care and authenticity, instead of hiding these needs to avoid disappointing others.

Balancing vulnerability and boundaries naturally supports emotional interdependence, where both partners feel free to rely on each other without losing their individuality. Non-codependent relationships involve moments of closeness and distance, sharing and privacy, openness and protection. This ebb and flow can feel uncomfortable at first, especially if old patterns trained you to either hold everything in tight or lose yourself in the relationship. But with patience and gentle practice, you can learn to welcome vulnerability as a strength and boundaries as acts of self-love.

Practically, implementing this balance may involve setting small, manageable goals. Start by identifying one or two personal boundaries that have felt blurred or ignored in past relationships. These might be around emotional topics you're not ready to discuss or times you need without interruption to process feelings. Share these boundaries with your partner or close friends in straightforward terms, inviting their understanding while reaffirming your commitment to the relationship. See how this honesty changes the dynamic. Most likely, it will invite deeper respect and safety.

At the same time, practice leaning into vulnerability in ways that feel low risk but meaningful. Share a hope or an insecurity with someone you trust and observe how it feels to be heard without pressure or judgment. Notice the difference between vulnerable moments that strengthen connection and those that feel unsafe or draining. These experiences will help you refine your boundaries and develop a keen sense for when it's right to open up and when it's okay to hold back.

Remember, vulnerability isn't a sign of dependency if it's grounded in a secure sense of self. It's about allowing yourself to be seen fully while being clear about what you will and won't tolerate. When boundaries and vulnerability coexist, you create a powerful foundation where intimacy can deepen without you losing your identity. This balance encourages healing from codependent patterns and lifts the quality of all your relationships.

Finally, it's essential to practice self-compassion along the way. Finding this balance isn't always easy. You might accidentally over-share or erect walls too high and shut people out temporarily. Both happen to everyone. What matters most is how you respond to these experiences—whether you judge yourself harshly or approach yourself with kindness and patience. Growth unfolds one step at a time, and each moment of vulnerability paired with healthy boundaries moves you closer to the freedom and confidence you're seeking in relationships.

Building Intimacy That Honors Both Partners

Intimacy is often portrayed as a seamless blending of two lives into one, but true intimacy honors both partners as whole, independent individuals. It thrives not by sacrificing personal needs or boundaries but by creating a space where vulnerability and respect coexist comfortably. This kind of intimacy doesn't happen by accident—it requires conscious effort to understand, appreciate, and uphold each person's sense of self. If you're striving to build stronger, healthier relationships, focusing on intimacy that honors both partners is essential for lasting connection.

One of the first steps in nurturing this kind of intimacy is recognizing that each person brings their own emotions, experiences, and desires into the relationship. It's tempting, especially for those recovering from codependency, to prioritize the other's feelings at the expense of their own. But intimacy deepens when both partners have the freedom to express authentic feelings without fear of rejection or judgment. This means creating an atmosphere where honesty is welcomed, even when it feels uncomfortable or challenging. True closeness is born from the courage to share inner truths alongside the willingness to listen deeply and empathetically.

Honoring both partners also means holding firm to personal boundaries while remaining open. Boundaries, far from creating distance, actually build trust by demonstrating respect for each individual's comfort zones and limits. When boundaries are clearly communicated and respected, partners feel safe to show up fully without losing themselves or feeling overwhelmed by the other's needs. This careful balance of connection and autonomy is the foundation of interdependence, where both individuals support one another's growth while maintaining their separate identities.

Communication plays a critical role in achieving intimacy that acknowledges and uplifts both partners. It requires more than just talking—it calls for active listening and a commitment to understanding. When both people feel heard and validated, it creates a feedback loop of connection that reinforces emotional safety. Vulnerability in this context isn't about exposing every insecurity but about sharing meaningful parts of oneself with the confidence that the other will respond with kindness and respect. It's this mutual exchange that transforms interaction into intimacy.

Developing this relational dynamic also involves self-awareness and emotional responsibility. Each partner must be willing to examine their own patterns and triggers that may interfere with intimacy. For example, past wounds and fears can unconsciously cause one to withdraw when they most need support, or to overstep boundaries in an attempt to control or feel secure. Recognizing these behaviors and choosing healthier responses strengthens the relationship. It shows a commitment to not only personal healing but also to the partnership's well-being.

Equally important is the practice of empathy—not just sympathizing with your partner, but truly understanding their inner world without rushing to fix or change it. When partners honor one another's experiences and feelings, even the difficult ones, it fosters an intimate connection rooted in acceptance rather than judgment. This environment allows both people to bring their full selves, including imperfections, to the relationship without fear of dismissal or punishment.

Another element that nurtures intimacy is shared vulnerability. While this might feel risky at first, sharing one's fears, hopes, and struggles can bridge emotional gaps and build closeness. Vulnerability invites a response of compassion, which in turn deepens connection. However, it's important that vulnerability is met with care and not exploited or dismissed. When intimacy respects and preserves each partner's emotional safety, it encourages ongoing openness rather than retreat.

Physical affection, when consensual and attuned to both partners' comfort levels, can also reinforce an intimate bond. But it's vital to remember that intimacy is not solely physical. Emotional and intellectual closeness matter just as much, if not more, for sustaining meaningful relationships. Intimacy is really about feeling deeply known and accepted in all dimensions.

Patience is a key ingredient as well. Building intimacy that honors both partners doesn't happen overnight. For many, especially those healing from codependent relationships, it's a gradual process of relearning how to be close without losing oneself. It requires ongoing effort to listen, respect boundaries, and offer support while holding firm to personal autonomy. Mistakes and misunderstandings will happen; what matters is the willingness to repair and recommit rather than shut down or retreat.

It's worth noting that honoring intimacy means making room for individuality—encouraging personal growth and interests outside the relationship. When both partners feel free to pursue their own passions and friendships, the relationship becomes a source of enrichment rather than restriction. This freedom fosters admiration and vitality, keeping the connection fresh and dynamic.

One practical way to cultivate intimacy that respects both partners is through regular check-ins that create space for honest conversation about feelings, needs, and boundaries. This kind of dialogue can help uncover unspoken assumptions or resentments before they build into larger conflicts. Check-ins don't have to be formal or lengthy—sometimes even brief moments of curiosity and openness are enough to reinforce connection and alignment.

Reflecting on your relationship's dynamics with awareness and compassion allows you to identify areas where intimacy might be falling short. Are both partners able to express themselves without fear? Do boundaries feel respected? Is vulnerability met with empathy rather than criticism? These questions can guide intentional growth toward deeper, more balanced intimacy.

Ultimately, intimacy that honors both partners is a practice of mutual respect, ongoing communication, and heartfelt vulnerability. It affirms that loving someone deeply doesn't mean losing yourself but rather choosing to intertwine your lives with kindness, trust, and authenticity. These relationships aren't just about avoiding unhealthy patterns; they're about embracing the full potential of connection where both people can thrive individually and together.

CHAPTER 20

Healing Through Forgiveness

Letting go of the pain that lingers from past relationship wounds isn't about excusing hurtful behavior but freeing yourself from its hold; forgiveness is a courageous act that opens the door to emotional liberation and growth. When you forgive, you're not rewriting history or denying your feelings — you're choosing to release resentment and cultivate peace within, which creates space for healthier connections moving forward. This process often starts with forgiving yourself for the decisions made when you were wounded, understanding that those choices were part of your journey rather than a reflection of your worth. Then, extending forgiveness toward others doesn't mean enabling harm or forgetting boundaries; instead, it means reclaiming your power by refusing to carry anger that weighs you down. Healing through forgiveness is a crucial step toward breaking free from codependent cycles, enabling you to step fully into interdependence with compassion, strength, and renewed hope for relationships that honor both yourself and those you care about.

Forgiving Yourself for Past Relationship Choices

One of the most challenging steps on the path to healing is learning to forgive yourself for the relationship choices you've made in the past. It's easy to get caught in a cycle of regret and self-criticism, especially when looking back at decisions that didn't turn out the way you hoped. But holding onto guilt or shame only keeps you stuck in patterns that prevent growth and true freedom. This kind of forgiveness isn't about excusing mistakes or pretending everything was perfect. Instead, it's about recognizing that you did the best you could with what you knew at the time, and allowing yourself to move forward with compassion and understanding.

When you start to forgive yourself, you create space for healing. Often, we treat ourselves harsher than anyone else ever would. We replay scenarios over and over, searching for the moment we "should have" acted differently. While reflection is part of learning, obsessing over past choices drains your energy and clouds your judgment. Forgiveness helps break this cycle. It's a conscious decision to stop punishing yourself and begin treating yourself as you would a close friend who's made mistakes. Imagine the kindness and patience you'd offer them—that's exactly what you need to extend inwardly.

Many people struggling with unhealthy relationship patterns carry a deep-seated fear that forgiving themselves means letting the past off the hook completely. But forgiving yourself doesn't mean erasing what happened. It's about embracing the whole experience, understanding the context behind your choices, and accepting that human beings are imperfect by nature. Sometimes your choices were influenced by wounds carried from childhood, misunderstandings about love and connection, or moments of emotional overwhelm. Acknowledging these influences isn't about making excuses; it's about offering clarity and compassion for what shaped you at each stage of your journey.

It helps to remember that growth isn't linear. You might forgive yourself one day and then feel self-critical again the next. That's normal. Healing through forgiveness is a process, not a destination you reach and stay at forever. In fact, even the most emotionally resilient people experience moments of doubt or second-guessing. What changes is how quickly you can recognize those moments and gently steer yourself back toward kindness. Over time, the habit of forgiveness reshapes your internal narrative—from one of blame to one of self-acceptance and empowerment.

One practical way to begin forgiving yourself is by revisiting the stories you tell yourself about past relationships. Often, those stories are loaded with shame, anger, or regret. Take time to write down what you believe about yourself in relation to those experiences. Are you calling yourself weak, foolish, or unworthy? Next, challenge those beliefs. Ask yourself if you'd say the same things to a good friend or family member who made similar decisions. More than likely, you'd offer understanding and encouragement. Reframe your story in a way that acknowledges your growth and the lessons learned. This shifts your mindset from punishment toward healing.

Sometimes, forgiving yourself requires addressing the guilt over not knowing better. We live in a culture that often values strength and perfection, which can make vulnerability feel like failure. But none of us enters relationships with a complete toolbox or full emotional vocabulary. Maybe you didn't recognize the red flags, maybe you stayed too long out of fear of being alone, or maybe you struggled to set boundaries because you didn't believe you deserved better. These aren't flaws; they're part of being human, and recognizing this allows you to practice patience and grace with yourself.

It's also important to remember that your past choices often led you to where you are now—a place of deeper self-awareness and desire for healthier connections. Without those experiences, the motivation to transform may not be as strong. This perspective helps turn what once felt like burdensome mistakes into stepping stones toward personal growth. Forgiving yourself doesn't erase the pain but transforms it into a catalyst for becoming the person who can build emotionally fulfilling, resilient relationships.

Forgiveness is an inside job. It's not about others giving you permission to move on or absolving them from their roles in your past difficulties. Even if a partner hurt or betrayed you, the first and most empowering forgiveness work happens within. When you release yourself from ongoing self-punishment, you create emotional freedom that opens the door for healthier interactions—with yourself and others. It's one of the most courageous and loving acts you can take on behalf of your future.

At times, the idea of forgiving yourself can feel overwhelming or even impossible. If so, start small. You might say affirmations such as "I am learning and growing," or "I forgive myself for not knowing then what I know now." These simple statements aren't empty platitudes—they're seeds of change. Repeating them regularly nurtures new ways of thinking about yourself and your relationship history. Pairing affirmations with practices like journaling or mindfulness can deepen your connection to self-compassion.

Another useful technique is to visualize yourself as the person you want to become—someone who sees their past with kindness rather than condemnation. Imagine embracing your younger self at moments when you made those decisions, holding them with warmth and understanding rather than judgement. Visualization can help rewire your emotional responses and soften feelings of shame or regret. It cultivates a sense of continuity within you, linking past and present with acceptance instead of conflict.

Healing through forgiveness also means recognizing that self-forgiveness is an ongoing commitment. It requires patience, honesty, and sometimes, professional support.

Therapy or counseling can provide the tools and guidance necessary to unpack complicated feelings and develop healthier self-perceptions. If you feel stuck in cycles of blame or guilt, reaching out for help is a powerful step toward reclaiming your emotional freedom.

Above all, be gentle with yourself during this process. Nobody expects perfection or demands instant transformation. Real change often comes from embracing the messiness of being human and moving forward despite it. Forgiving yourself frees up inner space to cultivate boundaries, boost self-worth, and build emotional resilience—all the qualities that give rise to the balanced, interdependent relationships you're working toward.

In time, as self-forgiveness deepens, you'll notice a shift in how you relate not only to your past but also to your present and future. You'll feel more equipped to make choices aligned with your genuine values and needs instead of old fears or patterns. The wounds left by unhealthy relationships won't disappear overnight, but they'll lose their grip on your sense of self. And that's where true healing begins—by loving and accepting yourself no matter what.

Approaching Forgiveness Toward Others Without Enabling

Forgiveness is often seen as the final step to healing difficult relationships and moving forward. But in the journey toward healthy interdependence, it's crucial to understand that forgiving someone does not mean allowing harmful behavior to continue unchecked. You can choose to forgive without enabling the very actions or dynamics that caused pain. The distinction is subtle but powerful—true forgiveness involves releasing resentment and anger without surrendering your boundaries or sense of self-respect.

One of the biggest challenges when learning to forgive others, especially in codependent or toxic relationship patterns, is the tendency to slip into enabling behaviors. This happens when forgiveness becomes a way to avoid confrontation or discomfort, effectively signaling to the other person that their harmful actions don't have consequences. It's easy to confuse forgiveness with acceptance of the status quo or blind tolerance, but those are not the same. Instead, forgiveness should be an active process that includes accountability and clear limits.

Many people who grew up in emotionally enmeshed families or relationships may have learned that protecting themselves meant trying to fix or smooth things over at all costs. Forgiveness, in that context, may have looked like ignoring red flags, excusing poor behavior, or taking responsibility for someone else's emotions. This pattern only entrenches unhealthy dynamics. Approaching forgiveness from the place of strength and self-awareness means you recognize where you end and the other person begins. It frees you to extend compassion without losing yourself.

To forgive someone without enabling them begins with a clear-eyed assessment of the situation. What behavior hurt you, and what boundaries were crossed? Were there patterns of manipulation, dishonesty, or disrespect involved? Holding onto forgiveness is not about denying this reality or ignoring your pain. In fact, forgiveness often takes the most courage when you allow yourself to fully feel the hurt first—acknowledging the impact honestly—before choosing to let go of bitterness. Suppressing emotions to fast-track forgiveness only leads to unresolved wounds and repeated cycles.

It also helps to redefine what forgiveness means to you personally. Forgiveness is not a gift you give the other person so they can feel better or continue as if nothing happened. Instead, think of forgiveness as reclaiming your own peace and emotional freedom. It's a decision to stop carrying resentment like deadweight. By letting go, you create space for healing and growth, both within yourself and in the relationship—if that relationship is healthy enough to move forward.

Forgiveness without enabling requires boundaries that protect your well-being. These boundaries are not walls built out of anger, but clear guidelines that communicate what you will and won't tolerate. For example, you might forgive a friend for past betrayals but still refuse to engage with them when they cross your limits again. Or you might find compassion for a partner's struggles but recognize that their refusal to seek help or change hurts you deeply and must be addressed firmly. Setting and enforcing boundaries keeps you grounded and prevents forgiveness from turning into self-sacrifice.

It's important to understand that forgiving doesn't mean reconciliation has to happen immediately—or ever. Sometimes, forgiveness is a private act performed in your own heart, without resuming contact with the person who caused harm. In fact, distancing yourself from toxic influences while working through forgiveness can be essential. It gives you the clarity and strength to heal without being pulled back into unhealthy patterns. Rebuilding trust should never be rushed or expected just because forgiveness has taken place.

Another key aspect of forgiving without enabling is developing emotional resilience. This means cultivating the ability to face difficult emotions and situations without falling into old habits like people-pleasing, appeasement, or blaming yourself for someone else's actions. Strong emotional resilience helps you respond to relational wounds with compassion—both for yourself and others—while maintaining your integrity. Practices like mindfulness, journaling, and therapy can be invaluable tools during this process.

When you forgive with healthy boundaries and resilience, you also open the door for accountability. Forgiveness can coexist with asking for what you need to feel safe and respected. It's perfectly valid—and often necessary—to express how someone's actions affected you and to communicate the changes you expect going forward. This isn't about demanding perfection or punishing someone; it's about creating the possibilities for healthier interactions, whether that means repair or parting ways.

One common concern is that holding someone accountable might undermine forgiveness or make you look unforgiving. The truth is the opposite. Accountability is an essential element of real forgiveness because it honors your worth and keeps toxic cycles from continuing. It sends a clear message: You forgive, but you will not be a passive participant in unhealthy dynamics. This stance encourages growth in both people and shows that forgiveness is a courageous, active commitment rather than a passive pardon.

Forgiving without enabling also invites a shift in focus—from trying to change others to focusing on your growth and healing. You can't control how someone else behaves or whether they choose to change. But you can control how you respond and what you allow into your life. This mindset empowers you to take responsibility for your emotional health and frees you from the exhausting burden of "fixing" others or situations. It's a shift from codependent rescue toward interdependent support.

It's normal to worry that holding firm to boundaries or insisting on accountability might create distance or conflict. But surrendering your boundaries to keep the peace often leads to more pain in the long run. Forgiveness lived out with strength helps you maintain relationships that are truly healthy or, if necessary, let go gracefully when a relationship cannot grow. This balance is essential for building connections that are mutual, respectful, and resilient.

In practice, approaching forgiveness involves ongoing self-reflection and self-compassion. It means checking in with yourself regularly: Are your boundaries being respected? Are you falling back into patterns of enabling? Are you allowing yourself to feel your true emotions rather than brushing them aside? It's a dynamic process, not a one-time event. Sometimes forgiving someone means repeatedly choosing peace over bitterness despite setbacks or disappointments.

Ultimately, forgiveness without enabling is an act of empowerment. It's a way to reclaim your agency and define your relationships on your own terms. When you practice this kind of forgiveness, you send a powerful message—to yourself and others—that you deserve respect, honesty, and kindness. You become a role model for healthy relational boundaries, showing that love and compassion don't require sacrificing your well-being. This approach lays the foundation for meaningful connections based on trust, honesty, and genuine care.

The road to forgiveness in the context of overcoming codependency and toxic patterns may feel challenging. But remember, it's possible to forgive without losing yourself. You can let go of the burdens of resentment and pain while still holding firm to what is true and right for you. In doing so, you nurture not only your own healing but also the possibility for healthier, more balanced relationships—ones that honor interdependence rather than unhealthy dependence.

CHAPTER 21

Self-Care Strategies for Relationship Health

Taking care of yourself isn't selfish—it's essential for fostering strong, balanced relationships. When you prioritize your well-being, you create a foundation that supports not just your own growth but also the health of your connections with others. This means carving out time to recharge, setting limits that protect your energy, and nurturing habits that keep you grounded emotionally and physically. Consistent self-care acts as a safeguard against slipping back into old codependent patterns by reinforcing your sense of worth and autonomy. Embracing these strategies empowers you to show up fully—clear, confident, and compassionate—

in all your relationships, laying the groundwork for mutual respect and true interdependence.

Prioritizing Your Well-Being Consistently

When you're working to build healthier relationships and break free from old, unhealthy patterns, one thing becomes clear: your own well-being can't be an afterthought. It needs to be a daily commitment, a steady foundation that supports every connection you make. Prioritizing your well-being consistently doesn't just mean occasional self-indulgence or last-minute de-stressing. It's about integrating self-care into your lifestyle so deeply that nurturing yourself becomes second nature, not a luxury or a guilty pleasure.

It's easy to fall back into people-pleasing habits or put your own needs aside, especially when you've spent years trying to maintain peace in chaotic relationships or avoid conflict. But sustained personal well-being acts like a protective barrier—it keeps you anchored, helps you respond instead of react, and empowers you to stay true to yourself. Without it, you risk losing the very autonomy and balance you're striving to regain. Prioritizing well-being consistently means treating yourself with the same kindness and respect that you want from others.

Start by recognizing well-being as a holistic concept. It's more than physical health or occasional pampering. Your emotional, mental, and spiritual health all need attention. For someone healing from codependency, emotional well-being might require ongoing work on recognizing emotional triggers and cultivating patience with yourself. Mentally, it might mean challenging negative self-talk and replacing it with affirmations that reinforce self-worth. Spiritually, whatever that looks like for you—whether meditation, nature, journaling, or a creative outlet—contributes to a balanced foundation for interdependence.

One obstacle many face is the misconception that prioritizing yourself feels selfish or self-centered. But self-care framed as selfishness is a misunderstanding. When you take consistent care of your needs, you actually enhance your ability to give and receive love in healthier ways. It helps prevent burnout, resentment, and emotional exhaustion—all of which sabotage relationship growth. In fact, the act of regularly prioritizing your well-being often models for those around you how self-respect and personal boundaries can look in action.

Building a routine around your well-being can seem daunting at first, especially if you've been accustomed to putting others first. A helpful approach is to start with small but consistent habits. These don't have to be elaborate or time-consuming. Simple practices like setting aside a few minutes in the morning for mindful breathing, journaling your emotions, or going for a short walk can make a big difference. The key lies in repetition and intention—showing up for yourself day after day.

And remember, what you need might shift as you deepen your healing journey. Some stages require more rest. Others need more energetic movement or creative expression. Checking in with yourself regularly is crucial for maintaining alignment with your well-being goals. This ongoing dialogue—

whether it's through meditation, reflection, or even talking it through with a trusted friend or therapist—keeps your self-care authentic rather than a box-checking exercise.

Part of prioritizing well-being consistently is understanding your personal limits and listening closely when you hit them. Pushing past emotional exhaustion or physical fatigue can feel productive in the short term, but it usually exacts a cost later. The challenge with codependency patterns is that you may have normalized ignoring discomfort to keep the peace or avoid abandonment. Unlearning this requires patience and recognizing that honoring your limits isn't weakness; it's strength and self-respect in practice.

It's also fundamental to establish boundaries that protect your well-being in everyday interactions. Clear boundaries aren't just about saying no—they're about clearly defining what you can and cannot accept in your relationships without compromising yourself. Boundaries become easier to uphold when your well-being is a priority because you aren't trying to negotiate your value or accommodate at your own expense. Instead, you invite a mutual respect that better supports a balanced connection.

Consistency is the secret ingredient that separates fleeting self-care moments from real transformation. It's one thing to indulge yourself on a rare day off; it's another to make well-being a consistent priority that shapes how you organize your time, energy, and attention every single day. Even on difficult days, when motivation lags or emotional turmoil hits, showing up—even in small ways—builds resilience. The cumulative impact of these daily choices eventually rewires old patterns of neglect and emotional fusion.

Of course, life will throw curveballs that challenge your well-being routine. Stressful periods, relationship conflicts, or unexpected crises can make self-care the first thing to fall by the wayside. That's precisely why consistency matters most—when the going gets tough, well-being habits offer a safety net. They anchor and comfort you, making it easier to cope without returning to codependent behaviors. It's the difference between reacting impulsively and responding thoughtfully to difficult emotions.

Another point worth highlighting is the role of community in sustaining well-being. While prioritizing yourself is an individual responsibility, it doesn't mean isolation or going it alone. Supportive relationships—whether friends, support groups, or professionals—complement your personal efforts. Being surrounded by people who respect your commitment to well-being can challenge old narratives of self-sacrifice and remind you that you deserve care. They can also provide accountability that keeps you consistent.

Equally important is learning to celebrate your wins, no matter how small. Progress in prioritizing well-being is rarely linear. Sometimes you'll have glowing successes and other times setbacks. When you honor each step forward, you reinforce positive momentum and build a sense of confidence in your ability to care for yourself. Celebrating wins shifts your focus from what you're "failing" at to what you're actively creating—a more balanced, joyful way of living.

Ultimately, prioritizing your well-being consistently is foundational for building the kind of interdependent relationships you want. It creates a space where you can engage authentically, maintain your sense of self, and contribute wholeheartedly without losing yourself. This isn't about perfection or never experiencing difficulty. It's about developing the ongoing commitment and compassion for your own needs that keep you grounded through life's ups and downs.

Taking care of yourself every day is both an act of healing and a radical statement of self-respect. It breaks the cycle of codependency by reminding you, again and again, that your well-being matters. And from this place of strength and balance, you'll find it easier to build relationships that honor both you and the people you love.

Tools to Prevent Relapse into Old Patterns

Breaking free from old relationship patterns isn't a one-time event — it's an ongoing process. Even after making significant progress toward healthier connections, the pull of familiar habits can sneak back in unexpectedly. That's why establishing concrete tools to prevent relapse plays a crucial role in sustaining relationship health. Without these tools, slipping into codependent tendencies or emotional fusion can feel like an inevitable return to square one, undermining all the growth you've accomplished.

The first tool you can cultivate is self-awareness. This isn't just about noticing when you feel triggered—that's important—but also being able to recognize the subtle shifts in your emotions and behavior that signal a creeping back toward old patterns. Keeping a regular check-in practice, such as journaling or self-reflection at the end of each day, helps build this awareness. For example, if you catch yourself people-pleasing or compromising your boundaries to avoid conflict, that's your cue to pause and reassess. When you can identify these moments early, you gain the chance to consciously choose a different response rather than react unconsciously.

Another powerful tool is cultivating a strong support network. Recovery from codependency isn't meant to happen in isolation—it thrives with connection and accountability. Trusted friends, therapists, or support groups can provide honest feedback when your behavior patterns start shifting back. Sometimes, it's hard to see our own blind spots, so having others who understand your journey can keep you grounded. They also offer encouragement during tough times, which helps prevent the feelings of loneliness or helplessness that often trigger relapse.

Developing clear, firm boundaries is an essential preventative strategy as well. Boundaries act as the guardrails that keep you from falling into patterns where you lose yourself in another's needs or emotions. However, boundaries aren't something you set once and forget; they require regular reinforcement. It's important to revisit your limits frequently—especially when stress is high or relationships become strained. If you notice a tendency to soften your boundaries to avoid conflict or maintain peace, that's a red flag. Using scripts or rehearsing boundary-setting conversations ahead of time builds confidence and reduces the chances of slipping back into old habituated behavior.

Emotional regulation skills are another indispensable tool in this toolkit. Codependent patterns thrive on emotional reactivity—usually driven by fear, anxiety, or the need for approval. Learning how to manage those feelings without losing control makes all the difference. Techniques like deep breathing, mindfulness meditation, or grounding exercises can interrupt the overwhelm that often leads to old, unhealthy responses. When you practice calming your nervous system in the moment, you create more space for reasoned, thoughtful decision-making—rather than impulsive actions that reopen wounds.

Part of preventing relapse also involves cultivating a growth mindset. Recognize that setbacks aren't failures; they're signals and opportunities to learn more about yourself. When you accept that change takes time and isn't perfectly linear, you reduce the shame and frustration that can perpetuate harmful cycles. Instead of beating yourself up for slipping, take a step back and analyze the situation with curiosity. What triggered the pattern? What feelings arose? What might help next time? This mindset shifts the narrative from "I can't do this" to "I'm growing, even through challenge."

In addition to internal tools, external reminders can reinforce new behaviors. Simple things like notes on your mirror, scheduled check-ins in your calendar, or apps that send motivational messages can help keep your intentions top-of-mind. Visual cues serve as gentle nudges that prompt you to stay on track, especially when daily life gets hectic. Creating rituals around your new relationship habits—whether it's a weekly reflection or practicing self-care routines consistently—builds healthy patterns that replace the old ones.

Accountability partnerships also contribute to long-term success. Partnering with someone else who's working on similar goals creates mutual motivation. You're not only accountable to yourself but to another person who cares about your well-being. Sharing your progress, challenges, and victories helps sustain momentum and keep you engaged in the healing journey. It's important that this relationship remains supportive, nonjudgmental, and balanced; otherwise, it risks becoming another codependent dynamic.

Equally vital is the practice of self-compassion. Often, relapse occurs because we judge ourselves harshly after a misstep. This internal criticism can spiral into feelings of unworthiness, which fuel old dependency needs. Choosing instead to treat yourself with kindness during moments of struggle quiets that inner critic and supports resilience. When you cultivate a compassionate inner voice, you reinforce your intrinsic value apart from your relationship behaviors or outcomes. This foundation of self-love makes it far easier to bounce back and try again.

Another tool to prevent slipping back is ongoing education and reflection. As we grow, new challenges arise that test our boundaries and emotional regulation. Keeping yourself informed about healthy relationships, attachment styles, and communication strategies provides fresh perspectives and keeps your skills sharp. Reading books, attending workshops, or engaging in therapy throughout your life ensures continuous improvement. The commitment to lifelong learning signals that healthy interdependence isn't a destination, but a journey that evolves over time.

It's also beneficial to create a personalized relapse prevention plan. This might include identifying specific triggers, drafting action steps for when emotions feel intense, and outlining people or practices to turn to for support. Having this plan laid out clearly removes guesswork when you're vulnerable. It acts as a safety net by giving you concrete tools ready to deploy before old patterns fully take hold. Revisiting and updating this plan as you grow keeps it relevant and effective through different phases of your healing.

Finally, embracing patience throughout this process strengthens all other tools. Healing and growth do not unfold overnight; they require time, effort, and intentionality. When you remember that setbacks are part of learning, you lessen the pressure and cultivate endurance. This patience allows you to meet each day with presence, giving yourself grace—not only for the progress you've made but for the ongoing work ahead. With persistence and the right tools, relapse becomes less frequent and less damaging, paving the way for deeper, more authentic connections.

CHAPTER 22

Embracing Independence Within Togetherness

Finding the balance between holding onto your independence while nurturing a deep connection with others is one of the most empowering steps on the path to healthy relationships. It means celebrating your personal growth without losing sight of the shared journey you're on, recognizing that true togetherness doesn't require sacrifice of self but rather opens space for both partners to thrive individually and as a unit. This delicate dance calls for ongoing awareness and intention—because independence within togetherness isn't a fixed destination; it's a dynamic, evolving practice that builds resilience and allows love to deepen without unnecessary dependency. When you embrace this balance, you reclaim your sense of self while creating a partnership grounded in mutual respect, trust, and freedom.

Celebrating Personal Growth Alongside Relationship Growth

One of the most profound shifts you can experience on the path from codependency to interdependence is discovering how personal growth and relationship growth can not only coexist but actually fuel each other. It's a dynamic dance where your individual journey toward emotional freedom and self-awareness becomes a source of strength and inspiration for your bond with others. Instead of feeling torn between nurturing your own development and supporting your partner or loved ones, you begin to celebrate progress made by everyone involved. This doesn't happen overnight, but appreciating this dual evolution sets a foundation for healthier, more resilient connections.

Think about how often people assume that relationship success means losing yourself to the couple or family identity. That old narrative suggests that to "make things work," you have to sacrifice parts of who you are. But when you embrace interdependence, you break free from that limited mindset. Growing as an individual—whether that means pursuing new goals, healing past wounds, or learning to communicate more honestly—is a gift to the relationship itself. When you're stronger and clearer within, you bring more authenticity and stability to the connection.

Recognizing personal achievement within the context of a relationship can be a cause for real celebration. Maybe you've set a firm boundary where before you might've said "yes" out of guilt. Or perhaps you've begun expressing your needs more openly, even when it felt scary at first. These are victories that highlight your growth and, in turn, deepen the trust and respect your partner has for you. The relationship becomes a space where evolving minds and hearts meet with kindness rather than judgment or fear. That kind of atmosphere encourages both people to keep moving forward, individually and together.

It's also important to understand that personal growth isn't a linear or predictable process. Sometimes, you'll take two steps forward and one step back. Other times, it might feel like you're stuck in place. Allowing yourself and your partner this kind of grace—that growth is messy and often nonlinear—builds resilience within your bond. When you celebrate the wins, no matter how small, you reinforce a pattern of positive encouragement instead of criticism. Remember, the goal isn't perfection; it's progress that matters.

Another piece of this celebration is learning to acknowledge and let go of unhealthy comparisons. When you're emerging from codependent patterns, it's easy to fall into the trap of measuring your growth against what you think a "perfect" relationship or person looks like. But interdependence is deeply personal and unique to every bond. By shifting away from comparison, you free yourself to appreciate the distinct ways that you and your partner grow. Maybe one day, it's about emotional vulnerability, and the next, one of you steps into more independence or self-care. Both paths are valuable.

Sharing milestones with your partner can deepen connection in powerful ways. Whether it's celebrating a breakthrough in communication or simply recognizing that you managed to stay grounded during a difficult conversation, marking these moments builds a shared history of growth. Creating rituals around these acknowledgments—like a weekly check-in or a small gesture of appreciation—helps transform growth from something internal and invisible into something tangible that strengthens your relationship. It reminds you both that you're on a shared journey, even as you maintain your individuality.

In healthy interdependence, maintaining your sense of self doesn't feel like a threat to the connection; it enriches it. As you grow, you get more comfortable with your emotions, boundaries, and needs. Your partner sees that you trust them enough to be authentic and that you respect yourself enough to stand firm when necessary. That balance breeds mutual admiration. You start to inspire each other, whether by pursuing individual dreams, engaging in new creative outlets, or confronting fears that held you back for years. The relationship becomes a safe place where growth isn't just accepted; it's honored.

One of the more subtle ways personal growth supports relationship growth is by enhancing emotional resilience. Developing skills like managing triggers, practicing self-compassion, and regulating difficult feelings reduces reactivity that can undermine connection. When you build these internal muscles, you contribute to a calmer, more grounded relational environment. Your partner benefits from that stability, and the partnership as a whole gains endurance to weather inevitable challenges. Growth here is less flashy but incredibly powerful—like tending to roots that support a flourishing tree.

But don't forget, growth happens individually, not just within the couple. Taking time to reflect on your personal progress—perhaps through journaling, therapy, or meditation—fortifies the foundation you bring when you're together. This inner work helps prevent falling back into codependent habits where emotional fusion clouds boundaries and self-trust. When you invest in yourself first, your relationship feels fresher and freer. You meet your partner as a whole person rather than a patchwork of past fears and unmet needs.

It's natural to want your partner to celebrate your growth too, but remember, their journey is their own. Sometimes their progress doesn't show up the same way or on the timeline you expect. Practicing patience and compassion when their growth looks different from yours is essential. This doesn't mean lowering standards or settling for less; it means recognizing that interdependence thrives on honoring uniqueness and timing. When both individuals find space to evolve without pressure, the connection holds more love and less tension.

Celebration isn't just about the big wins either. It's often the small, everyday moments that build momentum. Recognizing when you've communicated honestly instead of deflecting, or felt comfortable being vulnerable without shutting down, plants seeds of confidence. When these small acts of growth are acknowledged within your relationship, they compound over time and transform how you relate to one another. It's less about grand gestures and more about fostering a culture of encouragement that helps each person shine.

Furthermore, celebrating growth alongside your partner can deepen your shared sense of purpose. When two people commit to evolving—not just superficially but emotionally and spiritually—they craft a powerful narrative together. That narrative fuels motivation during tough times and enriches everyday life. It also builds hope, which is a critical ingredient in healing from codependency. Holding a vision where both partners flourish independently and together makes the relationship uplifting rather than draining.

At times, it's easy to forget that the relationship itself is a living, evolving entity. Just like individuals, it needs care, attention, and space to grow. Celebrating growth acknowledges the relationship's vitality and signals that it's worth investing in. This mindset helps break patterns of stagnation or resignation that can take root in codependent dynamics. Instead, you maintain forward momentum fueled by curiosity, kindness, and shared commitment.

In practical terms, incorporating celebration into your relationship might look like acknowledging when one of you takes on a new challenge, supports a boundary, or expresses feelings authentically. Maybe you create a habit of verbally affirming growth or write little notes of encouragement. These seemingly small practices accumulate, sending a clear message: growth matters and is valued here. Over time, this builds a positive feedback loop where both partners feel seen, supported, and motivated to keep evolving.

Ultimately, celebrating personal growth alongside relationship growth means embracing complexity and honoring change. It means letting go of old fears that independence threatens connection and replacing them with trust that your bond can grow stronger because of it. When you choose to celebrate the work you both put in—individually and together—you shift from codependency's limiting grip toward freeing, lasting interdependence. This celebration becomes a continuous source of hope, motivation, and love, lighting the way on your journey.

Maintaining Healthy Interdependence Over Time

Once the foundation of independence within togetherness is established, the real challenge begins: sustaining that balanced interdependence over the long haul. Healthy interdependence isn't a fixed state but a continuous process that requires attention, intention, and adaptation. Relationships, like people, evolve. What worked six months ago might not suit the partnership six years from now. Maintaining healthy interdependence means staying attuned to those changes without losing the individual sense of freedom and autonomy that each person rightfully deserves.

One vital aspect of nurturing this balance over time is embracing flexibility—not just as a concept, but as a daily practice. Life throws curveballs, circumstances change, and emotional needs fluctuate. Being rigid about how roles, responsibilities, or boundaries look can create tension. Instead, couples and close connections must approach these shifts with curiosity and openness. When both partners can check in honestly about where they're at emotionally and practically, they set the stage for ongoing mutual support without codependency creeping back in.

At the same time, maintaining healthy interdependence requires a strong commitment to self-awareness. It's tempting to get caught up in the daily rhythm of togetherness and lose sight of individual goals or feelings. Routine conversations with yourself—asking, "Am I still honoring who I am? Are my needs being voiced and respected?"—help keep the relationship anchored in authenticity. When either partner neglects their inner compass, the risk of slipping into unhealthy patterns such as emotional fusion or people-pleasing increases. Awareness acts as an early warning system, allowing course corrections before small cracks widen into unmanageable issues.

Alongside self-awareness, open communication remains a cornerstone. This goes deeper than just discussing schedules or surface concerns. It's about creating a safe space where vulnerability can be expressed without fear of judgment or rejection. Sharing not only joys but also disappointments, fears, and changes in personal desires strengthens trust and deepens intimacy. Over time, these transparent dialogues prevent misunderstandings and resentments from taking root, which often erode the solid foundation of interdependence.

Another critical factor in long-term interdependence is respecting and nurturing boundaries continuously. Boundaries aren't one-and-done declarations; they morph as people evolve individually and as a couple. For example, something that felt comfortable early in a relationship might later feel stifling or insufficient. Regularly revisiting and renegotiating boundaries creates clarity and reassurance. It's also a way to honor each partner's individuality while still holding space for togetherness. This ongoing boundary maintenance guards against enmeshment and ensures both parties feel seen and valued for who they truly are.

It's also worth noting that maintaining healthy interdependence means balancing dependence and independence naturally. It's normal to lean on each other during stress, major life events, or illness. What distinguishes healthy interdependence from codependency is how those moments are managed. Partners support one another without losing sight of their own identities or overstepping limits. This balance requires cultivating resilience individually, so support given doesn't morph into enabling or over-reliance, but rather becomes a genuine exchange of strength.

In the context of aging relationships, maintaining interests and friendships outside the partnership plays a powerful role in sustaining interdependence. Life enrichment comes from multiple sources—hobbies, friends, professional growth—which all feed into how individuals show up in their relationship. When one's sense of self depends solely on the partnership, the dynamic becomes fragile. Maintaining a rich personal life prevents emotional suffocation and fosters a healthier, more vibrant connection. Encouraging one another to thrive independently outside the romantic bond strengthens interdependence rather than threatens it.

Regularly practicing gratitude and appreciation also feeds the maintenance of healthy interdependence. Over time, familiarity can breed complacency or taken-for-granted attitudes. When partners intentionally acknowledge each other's contributions, efforts, and growth, it reinforces respect and admiration. These affirmations create a positive feedback loop that energizes the relationship and builds resilience against inevitable stresses and conflicts.

Healthy interdependence also relies on shared values and goals but allows for evolving perspectives. Aligning visions about major life choices—whether that's about finances, parenting, career trajectories, or lifestyle—creates a roadmap for moving forward together. But it's equally important to acknowledge that individual dreams might shift, too. When partners can support one another's evolving goals without feeling threatened or abandoned, the relationship grows deeper in trust and connection. This balance prevents power struggles and fosters a sense of partnership where both people feel free to evolve.

Forgiveness is often an overlooked ingredient in long-term healthy interdependence. No relationship is immune to mistakes, misunderstandings, or disappointments. Holding on to grudges or past hurts creates emotional barriers that constrict the flow of connection. Developing the capacity to forgive consciously—whether it's forgiving yourself or your partner—helps release toxic emotional weight. Forgiveness doesn't mean ignoring issues or enabling harmful patterns; instead, it's about choosing to move forward with a willingness to heal and rebuild, which is essential for enduring intimacy.

Another important part of maintaining this balance is learning to navigate conflict constructively. Conflict doesn't mean the relationship is failing; how conflicts are handled reveals the health of interdependence. Couples who can confront disagreements without escalating into blame or withdrawal create opportunities for growth and deeper understanding. It involves listening actively, seeking to understand before responding, and managing emotions so that resolution feels collaborative rather than combative. Over time, these practices build emotional safety and trust, even during challenging times.

Lastly, maintaining healthy interdependence over time involves celebrating both personal and shared milestones. Recognizing individual achievements alongside couple goals highlights that the relationship supports—not stifles—each person's growth. Whether it's a career promotion, a new hobby, or overcoming a personal hurdle, sharing those victories together reinforces connection and mutual pride. These celebrations serve as reminders that independence flourishes best within a nurturing partnership where both people cheer each other on consistently.

In summary, maintaining healthy interdependence isn't about perfect harmony or never facing difficulties. It's about committing to ongoing self-awareness, open communication, boundary renewal, and mutual respect. It means supporting one another's growth while holding firm to individual identity. When relationships are approached as living, breathing partnerships that evolve alongside each person, they become a source of freedom, strength, and deep connection—far from the trap of codependency. The journey isn't always easy, but the rewards reflect the effort: resilient bonds where both independence and togetherness shine equally and powerfully.

CHAPTER 23

Recognizing and Avoiding Relapse Triggers

It's easy to underestimate how subtle signs and familiar patterns can pull us back into unhealthy relationship habits, especially when we're emotionally vulnerable or stressed. Recognizing those relapse triggers—whether they're certain situations, emotional states, or old thought habits—is key to breaking the cycle and staying on a healthier path. When you learn to spot these warning signs early, you can create mindful action plans that shift energy away from reactive tendencies and toward intentional choices that honor your growth. This kind of awareness isn't about perfection but about catching yourself with compassion and steering back to interdependence, where both your needs and your relationships thrive.

Identifying High-Risk Situations and Mindsets

When it comes to breaking free from unhealthy relationship cycles, one of the most important steps is learning to recognize the situations and thought patterns that put you at risk of falling back into old habits. These high-risk moments don't always look dramatic or obvious. Sometimes, they sneak up in subtle ways—through a late-night phone call, a passing feeling of loneliness, or even a small challenge to your boundaries. Understanding these triggers is crucial because it allows you to prepare, respond thoughtfully, and protect your emotional well-being before damage happens.

High-risk situations often revolve around the familiar dynamics that originally fueled codependent behaviors. For instance, moments where you feel unheard or invalidated may push you to revert to people-pleasing or emotional merging. Times of vulnerability can make you crave connection so intensely that you minimize your own needs just to avoid feeling abandoned. You might be sitting with a partner or friend and catch yourself edging toward over-apologizing, or excusing behaviors that don't respect your boundaries. These subtle shifts signal that you're stepping into a zone where old patterns flourish.

While every individual's triggers will look a little different based on their personal history and relationship experiences, there are some common situations many people in recovery can recognize. Conflict is a classic example. When disagreements arise, it's tempting to either shut down, detach emotionally, or overcompensate by accommodating the other person excessively. Instead of healthy engagement, the knee-jerk reactions rooted in fear or insecurity take over. This isn't about blame—it's a survival strategy that your mind learned long ago. But now, awareness can provide a crucial pause, where you can choose a different response.

Certain environments also increase risk. Places or settings tied to past relationship trauma or emotional neglect might suddenly flood you with feelings that make self-protection nearly impossible. Being around people who tend to dismiss your feelings, or in scenarios where your needs routinely go unmet, can reawaken that inner codependent voice that says, "I just need to try harder" or "If I don't fix this, I'll lose them." Recognizing these external triggers helps you avoid falling into a reactive spiral.

Mindsets are a less visible but equally important piece of the puzzle. High-risk mindsets involve internal narratives, beliefs, and emotions that set the stage for relapse. For example, feeling unworthy or believing that your value depends entirely on others' approval can fuel the cycle repeatedly. These thoughts often come disguised as logical reasoning. You might find yourself thinking, "If I put their needs first, everything will be fine," or "I'm not lovable unless I'm constantly giving." They might seem harmless at first, but they quietly chip away at your self-respect.

Another dangerous mindset is rigid perfectionism—the idea that if you just "do it right," you can control the relationship outcome. When things inevitably don't go as planned, frustration and self-blame quickly follow. This can then reopen the door to reactive behaviors like emotional fusion or boundary erosion. Being able to catch yourself in this mindset and practice self-compassion instead makes a world of difference.

Feelings of loneliness and fear are powerful triggers too. At some point, almost everyone in recovery faces moments when they feel isolated or afraid of rejection. These emotions can cloud judgment and make the familiar but unhealthy patterns of seeking approval or merging feel like tempting quick fixes. The key is to recognize that loneliness is temporary and doesn't have to lead to relapsing into old habits. Developing strategies for sitting with discomfort instead of reacting can reinforce your emotional resilience.

It's also worth noting that high-risk situations can be linked to life transitions, like starting a new relationship, moving in together, or dealing with the loss of a relationship. Changes often disrupt the sense of stability you've worked hard to build, stirring up old insecurities. At these times, your reflex might be to abandon everything you've learned and revert to familiar patterns—for example, trying too hard to please or ignoring red flags. By identifying these stress points ahead of time, you can implement specific coping tools or reach out for support before slipping back occurs.

Social media and digital communication can present unique risks as well. Activities like scrolling through an ex's profile or sending overly frequent messages can feed anxiety and obsessive thinking. The instant availability of contact creates tempting opportunities to relive codependent dynamics—seeking reassurance, over-apologizing, or trying to "fix" misunderstandings immediately. Setting conscious boundaries around technology use is an important part of avoiding relapse in today's world.

One of the biggest challenges is that high-risk mindsets tend to operate beneath conscious awareness, so they require ongoing self-reflection to catch. Journaling, mindfulness practices, or discussing your feelings with a trusted friend or therapist can help shine light on these internal patterns. When you're able to see the habitual thoughts and emotions that usually trigger reactive behavior, you gain power over them. Instead of being swept under the current, you can choose your path mindfully.

Part of this process involves distinguishing between genuine care and the need to fix or control. Healthy interdependence is about sharing responsibility and honoring boundaries, not about overextending or losing yourself in another's emotions. High-risk moments often blur this line because they bring up the temptation to rescue or accommodate excessively. If you catch yourself slipping into excessive caretaking or sacrificing your well-being for the sake of harmony, it's a clear sign that you're in a danger zone.

On the flip side, isolation and avoidance can also be red flags. Pulling away completely from relationships in fear of being hurt can leave space for loneliness and negative self-talk to grow unchecked. It's important to find balance—engage in connection while holding firm to your boundaries and self-worth. Recognizing when avoidance may actually be protecting old fears rather than fostering real healing is a subtle but essential insight.

Ultimately, identifying your personal high-risk situations and mindsets is an act of self-respect and empowerment. It means taking responsibility for your growth without blaming yourself for the past. It also means giving yourself permission to feel vulnerable without guilt or shame. Remember, these high-risk moments aren't failures but invitations to deepen your self-awareness and build resilience.

As you continue on your journey toward balanced, healthy relationships, developing an ongoing practice of noticing these triggers and mindsets will become second nature. This awareness is like a mental safety net—catching you before you fall back into familiar but harmful patterns. The more clearly you know your danger zones, the stronger your capacity becomes to navigate them with grace and strength.

Action Plans for Staying on a Healthy Path

Moving forward after recognizing relapse triggers is a crucial step in creating lasting change. Staying on a healthy path means developing clear, practical strategies that help you remain grounded, even when old patterns try to sneak back in.

It's not about perfection but about consistent, mindful effort to protect your well-being and nurture relationships that honor your growth. These action plans focus on empowering you to build resilience, maintain self-awareness, and actively choose behaviors that support interdependence rather than codependency.

First, it's important to have a clear understanding of your personal warning signs—the subtle and obvious signals that indicate you're drifting toward old habits. These signals might be feelings of desperation to please, avoiding conflict at any cost, or sacrificing your needs for the comfort of others. Once you know what to watch for, you can catch yourself earlier and respond intentionally rather than react impulsively. Start by creating a personal checklist of your common triggers and emotional patterns. Place this somewhere visible, like your journal, phone notes, or a mirror. This list serves as a quick reminder to pause and assess when situations feel overwhelming or confusing.

Another vital element is establishing and maintaining healthy boundaries. Boundaries are the guardrails that keep you safe and connected to your core self. When you find those boundaries starting to blur, it's a sign to re-center and reinforce what you need to feel respected and heard. A strong boundary practice includes regularly checking in with yourself to evaluate if you're saying yes out of genuine interest or out of obligation. It takes courage to say no sometimes, but this act of self-care preserves your energy and nurtures mutual respect in your relationships.

Building a support network is equally important. Change doesn't happen in isolation. Surround yourself with people who understand your journey and encourage your growth. This can include trusted friends, family members, therapists, or support groups focused on healthy relationships. Having these allies provides perspective and accountability, especially during challenging moments when relapse risks are heightened. When you feel the urge to revert to codependent patterns, reaching out instead of retreating can make all the difference.

Mindfulness and self-reflection form the backbone of sustained progress. Daily habits like journaling, meditation, or simply sitting with your thoughts give you space to process emotions and observe your reactions without judgment. Consistent self-awareness helps you identify when you're slipping back into familiar, unhealthy responses. It's normal for setbacks to happen, but what matters is how you respond to them. Take these moments as opportunities to learn more about yourself rather than reasons to feel shame or defeat.

Incorporating emotional regulation techniques enhances your ability to remain steady amid relational turmoil. Practices such as deep breathing, grounding exercises, or visualization help you pause before reacting. These tools allow you to respond thoughtfully instead of falling into reactive habits that disrupt connection. Over time, these calming strategies become second nature, making it easier to navigate emotionally charged situations without losing your sense of self.

Another key part of staying on track is focusing on your personal goals beyond relationships. Developing interests, cultivating hobbies, and investing in areas that bring you joy and fulfillment keep your identity strong. When your sense of self stands on its own foundation, relationships become a source of enrichment, not dependency. Designing a life that reflects your values and passions protects you from slipping into codependent dynamics where you sacrifice your well-being for others' approval.

Creating daily routines that prioritize self-care proves invaluable. This doesn't have to mean elaborate rituals but small, consistent actions like getting enough sleep, eating nourishing foods, moving your body, or setting aside quiet time. These routines build physical and emotional resilience, keeping you better equipped to handle relational stressors. Also, learning to celebrate your progress, no matter how small, reinforces positive change. Acknowledging your efforts strengthens motivation and boosts your confidence in navigating relationships with balance.

Technology can serve as a helpful tool if used mindfully. Setting reminders for check-ins, using apps for journaling or meditation, and joining online communities focused on healthy relationship building provide accessible resources anytime you need encouragement. However, it's important to avoid scrolling through social media or engaging with content that triggers insecurity or comparison. Being intentional about your digital environment keeps your focus on growth instead of distraction.

Practice patience and kindness toward yourself during times of struggle. The path away from codependency is often uneven and challenging. Expecting instant results sets you up for frustration. Instead, adopt a mindset of gradual improvement and compassion. Recognize that slipping back occasionally does not erase your progress—it provides clarity on areas that need more attention. Compassionate self-talk fosters resilience and helps you maintain momentum rather than giving in to discouragement.

Finally, revisit your "why" regularly—the deeper reasons behind your commitment to healthier relationship patterns. Whether it's to build safer connections, experience genuine intimacy, or reclaim your autonomy, keeping these motivations front and center fuels your determination. Write them down, remind yourself when it feels hard to stay strong, and let this purpose steer your choices. Aligning your daily actions with your core values strengthens your foundation for lasting change.

Remember, action plans aren't about rigid rules but flexible guides that shift with your needs and circumstances. Check in with yourself periodically to adjust strategies as you grow, and stay open to learning new approaches. Each step you take toward healthier patterns is a victory. Over time, these intentional practices weave into your life, making balanced, interdependent relationships not only possible but natural.

CHAPTER 24

CREATING A VISION FOR YOUR RELATIONSHIP FUTURE

As you step into this chapter, it's time to look ahead and intentionally shape what you want your relationships to be—a future where mutual respect, emotional balance, and authentic connection thrive. Creating this vision means peeling back old narrative layers shaped by codependency and crafting goals that honor your growth and freedom. It's about imagining partnerships, whether romantic or platonic, that nourish your individuality while inviting deep interdependence, where both people feel seen, valued, and free to express their true selves. This vision acts as your compass, guiding decisions and interactions that support healthy patterns instead of repeating old cycles. Remember, it's not about perfection but progress—building a relationship future that feels sustainable, loving, and resilient, with foundations rooted in trust, self-awareness, and shared values.

Setting Goals for Balanced, Loving Connections

As you start imagining what a healthy, interdependent relationship looks like for you, setting clear goals becomes essential. Goals act as a compass, guiding your efforts toward cultivating connections that are genuinely balanced and loving. Without defined intentions, it's easy to slip back into old, codependent habits or settle for less than you deserve. When you approach relationships with purposeful goals, you give yourself permission to expect and create emotional safety, mutual respect, and authentic closeness.

Setting goals for balanced connections first means understanding what balance looks like on a personal level. Balance is not about perfection or equal effort in every moment; rather, it's about maintaining a dynamic where both partners feel seen, heard, and valued. This can mean different things depending on the relationship. For example, one relationship may thrive with more open emotional sharing, while another needs stronger boundaries to flourish. Identifying what balance means for you sets a foundation that supports emotional freedom without losing connection.

When crafting these goals, it helps to reflect on your past relationship patterns—what felt safe and nourishing, and what triggered your need to people-please or lose your sense of self. Awareness of these patterns allows you to set goals that challenge unhealthy dynamics rather than unknowingly reinforce them. For instance, if you often found yourself suppressing your feelings to keep peace, a powerful goal might be to speak up honestly and compassionately when something bothers you, even if it feels uncomfortable at first.

Emotional safety is a central pillar in balanced relationships and deserves its role as a key goal. This means both you and the people you care about cultivate environments where vulnerability is met with kindness instead of judgment. Setting goals around creating and maintaining emotional safety requires practicing patience, choosing empathy, and developing skills like active listening and gentle honesty. These goals might initially seem abstract, but they manifest in daily interactions—how you respond during conflict, how you share your hopes and fears, and how you support each other's growth.

Another crucial aspect to include in your goal setting is mutual respect. Respect in an interdependent relationship is not just about honoring each other's boundaries but also valuing differences in perspectives, needs, and rhythms. Setting goals around respect encourages you to protect your own dignity while simultaneously uplifting your partner's. This could look like agreeing to disagree without blame, or committing to regular check-ins that honor each person's emotional state and energy levels. Goals that nurture respect help create a balanced partnership, where both people feel empowered rather than diminished.

Clear communication often stands out as a top priority when setting relationship goals. Without it, even the best intentions can fall apart because misunderstandings grow and resentments fester. Building goals around expressing your needs, desires, and limits with clarity helps avoid emotional confusion and codependent cycles. One goal could be to practice assertiveness skills, where you articulate what you want confidently without aggression. Another might focus on improving listening skills to ensure that your partner feels genuinely heard and understood. These goals aren't just about talking more—they're about creating space for heartfelt connection that honors both parties.

It's essential to approach goal-setting with flexibility and self-compassion. Relationships are living, breathing entities, and so are you. What feels like a reasonable goal today might need revisiting as you evolve personally and with your partner. Sometimes progress will feel slow, and setbacks may happen, but that doesn't mean failure; it simply means you're growing. Setting goals as flexible guideposts rather than rigid rules encourages resilience and adaptability—key qualities for long-term relationship health.

Part of this flexibility involves recognizing when a goal needs support. A balanced and loving connection rarely happens in isolation. You might find that some goals require help—whether it's therapy, trusted friends, or support groups—to break free from patterns that have held you back. Setting goals with awareness of needing occasional support is a strength, not a weakness. It shows you're actively investing in your growth and opening the door to deeper, more authentic relationships.

Building emotional resilience ties closely with your goals for relationship balance as well. When you aim to cultivate a connection that honors both your independence and intimacy, resilience becomes the buffer that absorbs inevitable stress without damaging your bond. Goals can include developing personal coping strategies, learning to manage triggers, and staying grounded even when your partner struggles or relationship challenges arise. This resilience strengthens the trust you place in yourself and in your ability to navigate tough moments without falling back into old codependent behaviors.

Setting goals for balanced, loving connections also invites you to clarify what you want less of in your relationships. Sometimes the most powerful goals describe what you don't want—a connection marred by guilt-tripping, manipulation, or emotional erosion. Being clear about what you're unwilling to tolerate creates boundaries that protect your well-being and reinforce healthy patterns. Goals like "I want to refuse emotional manipulation without guilt" or "I want to notice when I'm losing myself and stop it early" set a proactive standard for emotional health.

It's worth remembering that these goals don't only apply to romantic relationships. The skills, awareness, and expectations you set transfer to friendships and family ties as well. Healthy interdependence is about maintaining good emotional hygiene in all close connections, making it easier to engage authentically and safely with the people around you. So, your goals might include fostering honesty with your siblings, or practicing saying no to friends when you need space. Keeping your broader relational ecosystem in mind makes your efforts more sustainable and rewarding.

One of the most transformative aspects of goal-setting is that it shifts your role in relationships from reactive to proactive. Instead of feeling like a passenger caught in others' emotional tides, you become an active participant shaping the connection according to your values and needs. This presence of mind encourages you to prioritize your healing and growth not as acts of selfishness but as essential ingredients for love that lasts.

Finally, keep in mind that setting goals is not about rushing to an end point but about creating a vision that inspires ongoing effort and curiosity. Balanced, loving connections evolve, deepen, and sometimes challenge us. Goals serve as reminders of what you're building—relationships where you can show up fully without losing yourself, where intimacy and independence coexist, and where love is a source of strength rather than depletion. Approaching this process with patience and kindness ensures that your commitment to healthy connection becomes a gift you give yourself every day.

Building Support Systems That Reinforce Growth

Creating a vision for your relationship future can only go so far without the foundation of strong support systems.

These systems don't just support your relationships—they actively reinforce the growth you want to see within yourself and your connections. Too often, people trying to move past codependency believe they can or should do it alone. The reality is, lasting change thrives within community and reliable support. Whether that's friends, family, mentors, or professional help, the people and resources we surround ourselves with influence our ability to maintain balance, set boundaries, and deepen intimacy.

Building these support systems doesn't mean you're dependent or weak. Instead, it reflects an important lesson in interdependence—a healthy give-and-take that nurtures both your own well-being and your relationships. Think of your support system as the backbone that upholds your commitment to growth even when things get challenging. It holds space for honest conversations, offers encouragement when you stumble, and serves as a reality check when self-doubt creeps in.

At the core, reinforcing your growth through support begins with assessing who's in your circle and recognizing whether those relationships nurture or drain your energy. This can be tricky to navigate for those who've spent years caught in patterns where codependent habits blurred boundaries and shifted focus away from self-care. Identifying individuals who genuinely respect your boundaries and encourage your independence allows you to foster connections built on mutual respect.

Sometimes this means consciously stepping back from relationships that reinforce old unhealthy habits, even if that feels uncomfortable. Growth often demands letting go of what no longer serves us, including people. Although painful, this intentional pruning makes room for new kinds of support to enter your life—the kind that uplifts, challenges, and holds you accountable without judgment. Friendship and support networks should empower, not limit, your journey toward healthier connections.

Online communities and support groups can play an essential role here. For many, finding others who understand the struggle of codependency and the desire for relational balance creates a safe environment to share experiences and tools. These spaces validate your feelings and remind you that change is possible, which can be crucial during moments of isolation or setback. Don't underestimate the power of belonging to a group that's walking a similar path—it reduces shame and cultivates motivation to keep moving forward.

Professional support is another pillar that solidifies growth. Therapists, counselors, or coaches who specialize in codependency and healthy relationship dynamics provide tailored insights and skill-building techniques. They can help you spot unconscious patterns that might be hard to recognize on your own and offer guidance when you face emotional roadblocks. Investing in this type of support signals a clear commitment to yourself and your relational health. It's an act of self-respect that reinforces your vision by giving you tools to navigate challenges thoughtfully.

Equally important is cultivating allies within your immediate life who can hold you accountable in everyday moments. This might be a friend who gently reminds you to practice boundaries or a family member who celebrates your progress instead of reinforcing old narratives. You need people who see the real you, without trying to fix or control, and encourage your authentic self-expression without fear. These connections fuel confidence and give you the courage to keep redefining old relationship patterns.

Of course, support systems aren't just about receiving help; they also thrive when you actively contribute back. Interdependence isn't one-sided. Sharing your own experiences and support helps create reciprocal relationships, which deepen bonds and provide a richer sense of belonging. When you offer your time, empathy, or encouragement, you reinforce your growth by stepping out of the isolation codependency often fosters. This active engagement supports not just your partners or friends but yourself as well.

Establishing routines that strengthen your emotional well-being within these support systems can be transformative. Regular check-ins with trusted people, whether in person or virtual, offer ongoing feedback and celebrate milestones. It also lets you practice communicating openly about your needs, challenges, and boundaries in a safe context. These consistent interactions build emotional resilience by normalizing vulnerability and honesty in relationships.

Another practical aspect to consider is broadening your sources of support beyond the personal. Books, podcasts, workshops, and online courses provide valuable information and fresh perspectives. They act like mentors available on-demand, allowing you to learn and reflect independently while reinforcing the lessons you gain from personal connections. Curating a diverse mix of support channels deepens your understanding of interdependence and equips you with a variety of approaches to apply in different situations.

At times, you might face resistance or skepticism from those around you, especially if they're unfamiliar with interdependence or think of relationships only through traditional or codependent lenses. Handling this requires patience and clear communication about your boundaries and goals. You don't need to convince everyone to join your journey—instead, focus on sustaining relationships that embrace and respect your vision. The courage to stand firm in your healing process strengthens your sense of self and signals those around you that you're serious about change.

It's also worth acknowledging the role of self-support within this system. While external connections are vital, the ability to be your own steady source of encouragement can make all the difference. Self-support practices like journaling, meditation, or affirmations serve as internal anchors when external support isn't immediately available. Developing this inner resilience ensures you don't swing back into old patterns of emotional dependency during difficult times, but instead, can sustain your growth independently.

In the long run, support systems that reinforce growth mirror the qualities you want in your relationships: trust, respect, balance, and mutual empowerment. When you invest in cultivating and maintaining these connections, they become living proof that healthier relational patterns are possible. They testify to the power of community in healing and the strength found in asking for help and giving it back.

The process isn't static. Your support system will evolve as you grow, just like your relationships. Some connections will deepen, others will fade, and new ones will emerge. Stay open to this fluidity and trust that with each intentional step, you're creating a relational environment capable of sustaining your vision of balanced, loving, and interdependent connections. The journey to freedom from codependency isn't meant to be a solo road—it's a networked path, bolstered by people and practices that help you thrive.

CHAPTER 25

Becoming an Advocate for Healthy Relationships

Stepping into the role of an advocate for healthy relationships means more than just changing your own patterns—it's about using your experience and growth to inspire others on their journeys. By openly sharing what you've learned, you help dismantle the stigma around codependency and foster a community where emotional well-being is valued and nurtured. Advocacy can take many forms, from listening with empathy to those still struggling, to guiding friends or family toward healthier ways of connecting, or even participating in broader conversations about relationship health. As you embrace this role, you become a catalyst for change, helping to create spaces where balanced, interdependent bonds thrive, reminding others that healing and growth are both possible and worthwhile. This chapter encourages you to recognize the power in your story and the positive impact your voice can have in building a future where healthy relationships are the norm.

Sharing Your Journey to Inspire Others

There's a profound power in sharing your personal story of healing and growth. When someone steps forward to reveal their journey from codependency to healthy interdependence, it lights a path for others feeling lost in similar struggles. Your experience becomes more than just a chapter in your life; it transforms into a beacon of hope and guidance for those who need it most. This kind of sharing isn't about perfection or having all the answers. It's about honest, vulnerable storytelling that says, "You're not alone, and change is possible."

Opening up about the challenges you've faced may feel daunting at first. After all, old patterns of shame and secrecy can whisper loud messages about hiding pain or failure. But choosing to voice your story breaks down those walls and invites authentic connection. It reminds both you and others that vulnerability is a strength, not a weakness. With every part of your journey you share, you contribute to dismantling stigma around emotional struggles and unhealthy relationships—helping pave the way for more people to seek healing and support.

When sharing, it's helpful to focus not only on the hardships but also the small victories and lessons learned along the way. Highlighting the moments of self-discovery, boundary-setting, and increased self-worth can inspire others to believe these milestones are within their reach too. Growth in relationships isn't linear or flawless; it's a fluid process with ups and downs that require patience and perseverance. By painting this honest picture, you set realistic expectations for those working on their own healing journeys.

Everyone's path looks different, but the core experiences of pain, hope, and resilience connect us all. Your unique story adds richness and variety to the collective understanding of what it takes to transform damaging patterns into balanced, loving relationships. When you share honestly, you help normalize the very real struggles many people face behind closed doors. This normalization can relieve feelings of isolation and shame, making it easier for others to reach out for help.

Technology offers powerful platforms to amplify your voice, whether through blogging, social media, podcasts, or community forums. Finding or creating safe spaces where your message can be shared openly encourages a network of mutual support. These digital communities often become sources of encouragement and accountability, nurturing growth on both sides—those who share and those who listen. At the same time, in-person support groups or speaking engagements can foster deeper, face-to-face connections that reinforce empathy and understanding on a very personal level.

Mindful sharing requires thoughtful consideration about boundaries. It's important to decide ahead of time how much you're comfortable revealing and to protect your emotional well-being throughout the process. Sharing your story doesn't mean you owe everyone every detail of your life. Instead, it's about speaking from a place that feels safe and authentic. Respecting your own limits models healthy boundary-setting for others and prevents burnout or retraumatization.

As you become more comfortable with sharing, you might discover unexpected benefits. Many find that their stories create meaningful conversations with friends, family, or even strangers—conversations that spark new awareness and positive change across various relationships. The ripple effect of your courage to be open can touch countless lives, far beyond what you may initially imagine. It shows how individual transformations contribute to a larger cultural shift toward emotional health and genuine connection.

Being an advocate for healthy relationships doesn't require formal titles or professional credentials. It starts with the willingness to speak your truth and hold space for others' stories as well. You become part of a growing movement that values self-respect, empathy, and balanced connection over dependency and control. Your voice helps rewrite the narrative from one of struggle and isolation to one of empowerment and shared growth.

It's also worth recognizing that sharing your journey invites continued growth for yourself. Explaining your experiences to others often clarifies your own understanding and rebuilds self-worth through witnessing the positive impact of your story. Many people describe feeling a renewed sense of purpose and motivation when they realize their past pain has become the foundation for inspiring hope. In this way, advocacy becomes both an outward and inward act of healing.

As your advocacy evolves, consider combining your story with practical tools or insights you've found helpful. Offering actionable steps alongside your experiences equips others with concrete ways to start their healing process. Whether it's recommending books, sharing journaling prompts, or guiding boundary exercises, these resources complement your narrative and empower listeners to take meaningful action. This approach makes your advocacy not only heartfelt but also highly useful.

Healing from codependency often involves rebuilding trust—not only in others but also in yourself. Your openness encourages others to start trusting their own instincts and capacity for change. The courage you demonstrate in sharing fosters a culture where emotional struggles can be met with understanding rather than judgment. This culture shift is vital in breaking cycles of unhealthy relating that get passed down through generations.

Remember, you don't have to have arrived at the finish line to be a powerful advocate. Sharing your ongoing journey, including setbacks and vulnerabilites, can resonate even more deeply. It's a reminder that growth is a lifelong process and that everyone deserves grace, patience, and encouragement along the way. When you embrace your story in its entirety, it becomes a source of strength and connection for yourself and others.

Ultimately, your willingness to share transforms isolation into community and silence into dialogue. It unlocks the potential for collective healing grounded in real human experience. By becoming a voice for healthy relationships, you inspire a future where interdependence rests on mutual respect, self-awareness, and emotional resilience. Your journey is invaluable, and sharing it is one of the most courageous acts you can take toward building a better world for yourself and those around you.

Resources and Communities for Continued Support

Embarking on the journey toward healthy, interdependent relationships often feels like stepping into unfamiliar territory. While the insights and tools you've gathered so far are invaluable, sustained growth rarely happens in isolation. Support networks—both professional and peer-based—can provide the encouragement, validation, and guidance needed to navigate challenges that pop up along the way. Finding the right resources and communities becomes a crucial part of not only maintaining what you've built but also deepening your understanding of yourself and your relationships over time.

One of the strongest foundations for continued healing and empowerment comes through connecting with others who share similar experiences or goals. Community doesn't always mean large groups; it can be as simple as a close-knit support circle where people hold space for one another without judgment. Being part of such circles often lifts the heavy burden of feeling misunderstood or alone when old patterns arise. It's powerful to witness others' journeys, celebrate wins, and learn from setbacks without the pressure of perfection. This kind of shared vulnerability makes the path less daunting.

Online forums and support groups specifically focused on codependency and interdependence have become incredibly accessible and diverse. Platforms like specialized discussion boards, social media groups, or apps dedicated to mental health communities offer a chance to reach out anytime you're feeling stuck or overwhelmed. The tricky part, however, is finding groups that promote healthy, growth-focused conversations instead of enabling old behaviors or negativity. Many communities have moderators or guidelines designed to cultivate respectful and supportive environments. When you find these spaces, they can become integral to reinforcing the work you're doing in your day-to-day life.

Professional support also plays its role alongside peer groups. Therapists, counselors, and coaches trained in relationship dynamics and codependency offer tailored support that's often essential for unraveling deeply ingrained patterns. If you haven't yet explored professional help, it's worth considering as an ongoing resource—not just as a crisis tool but as a consistent partner in your journey. Even periodic check-ins can help you stay grounded, sharpen your self-awareness, and troubleshoot relational concerns before they escalate.

Workshops and retreats focused on interdependence, emotional resilience, or boundary-setting provide unique opportunities that blend education with hands-on practice. These events often encourage participants to step outside their comfort zones in a safe, structured way while surrounded by empathetic peers and expert facilitators. Whether it's a weekend seminar or a longer immersive retreat, these settings can accelerate learning and create bonds that last well beyond the event itself. Investing time in these experiences can be a turning point that reignites motivation and renews your commitment to your relational health.

Books and literature continue to be timeless companions in this work. While you've likely explored many recommended reads already, this field is constantly evolving, with fresh perspectives emerging all the time. Authors who write from a place of lived experience, clinical expertise, or both, often provide new insights or techniques that resonate on a different level depending on where you are in your journey. Revisiting foundational texts alongside more recent publications can offer both reassurance and inspiration as you deepen your understanding of interdependence.

Podcasts and online videos are another growing resource, especially for those who prefer consuming content in a more flexible or accessible format. Hearing stories from others who have navigated codependency, listening to experts break down complex topics, or gaining practical tips on communication and boundaries can reinforce everything you're working toward. Subscribing to a handful of trusted channels or series keeps this support at your fingertips, whether you're on a morning walk or winding down after a long day.

Spiritual or mindfulness communities can also support your relationship growth, especially if you gravitate toward practices that anchor emotional regulation and self-compassion. Meditation groups, yoga classes, or faith-based gatherings, when aligned with your values, provide additional layers of support that nourish your inner world. These spaces often emphasize presence, acceptance, and non-judgment, which directly counteract the shame and self-criticism common in codependent patterns. Integrating mindfulness or spirituality into your support network can profoundly complement the more cognitive or behavioral strategies in this work.

Family and close friends can be part of your support system too, though this depends heavily on your unique circumstances and their willingness to respect your boundaries and growth. Sometimes loved ones don't fully understand codependency or interdependence, which can create challenges. In these cases, patience and clear communication about your needs are key. Sharing with trusted individuals who can listen without trying to "fix" you or judge your progress can be a comforting anchor. If your current relationships don't offer this, developing friendships with new, like-minded people through community events or interest-based groups can fill that gap.

Local community centers and nonprofit organizations often host support groups and educational sessions related to healthy relationships and emotional wellness. These resources tend to be more affordable or even free, making them accessible for many people. They also provide the added benefit of face-to-face interaction, which can be invaluable when trying to build trust and receive real-time feedback. Checking local listings or community bulletin boards may reveal hidden gems you hadn't considered yet.

It's important to remember that not every resource or community will be the right fit, and that's okay. Sometimes, discovering where you feel safe and understood involves trial and error. The goal isn't to become dependent on any single group or source but rather to build a varied network of support that you can lean on when life gets complicated. Your needs may change over time, and allowing yourself the flexibility to step in and out of different communities as you evolve shows resilience and self-respect.

When joining any group or seeking new support, trust your instincts. Does this place or person make you feel heard, valued, and safe? Do they encourage your autonomy and growth rather than foster reliance or shame? These questions matter deeply. The best resources will honor your individual path and promote empowerment, not perfection or conformity. Remember to guard your boundaries even within supportive communities; your well-being comes first in every interaction.

Sharing what you learn with others is one of the most powerful ways to sustain your own growth and help others along their paths. Whether it's through volunteering, peer mentoring, blogging, or informal conversations, advocacy not only spreads awareness but reinforces your own commitments and wisdom. Becoming a voice for healthy relationships strengthens the fabric of community and reminds you that your journey has purpose beyond yourself. It's a beautiful cycle—supporting others energizes your own healing and vice versa.

In the end, resources and communities aren't just lifelines; they're catalysts. They drive transformation by reminding you that freedom from unhealthy patterns is possible—and that no one is meant to walk this road alone. Keeping your heart open to these connections, while honoring your personal boundaries, creates a powerful foundation for lasting change. With the right support at your side, the vision of interdependent relationships moves from hopeful idea to everyday reality.

EMBRACING INTERDEPENDENCE AS A LIFELONG JOURNEY

Stepping into the world of interdependence isn't about reaching a final destination or checking a box. It's an ongoing, evolving journey that reshapes how you relate to yourself and others day by day. After moving through the twists and turns of overcoming codependent patterns and building healthier connections, you come to appreciate that interdependence requires commitment—not just to another person but to your own growth, healing, and authenticity. It's not about perfection; it's about showing up with openness, honesty, and courage, even when it feels messy or uncertain.

The idea of being interdependent can sometimes feel intimidating because it demands vulnerability paired with strength. It asks you to stand firmly in your sense of self while leaning into the support and presence of others. This delicate balance, once mastered, creates bonds that nourish rather than drain, that build rather than break. Remember, this balance isn't static. There will be phases when you need more independence and others when leaning into connection makes the most sense. Honoring that ebb and flow honors your humanity and cultivates resilience.

Walking this path means recognizing that setbacks aren't failures but opportunities to deepen your understanding of yourself and your relationships. Old habits or emotional reflexes may resurface from time to time—it's natural. In those moments, leaning into the tools and insights you've gathered throughout your journey can help you regain footing and move forward more wisely. Self-compassion is your anchor here. When you respond to yourself with kindness instead of criticism, you create the fertile ground needed for lasting change.

One powerful realization in embracing interdependence is that freedom and connection aren't opposites but intertwined aspects of healthy relationship living. Many who have struggled with codependency may have believed that closeness meant losing oneself, or that independence required shutting others out. Interdependence shatters those myths. It invites a new way of being—where freedom thrives within connection, and connection deepens through respect for each individual's autonomy.

As you continue to nurture emotional responsibility, you'll notice the joy that comes from trusting both your capacity to take care of yourself and your ability to receive care from others. This mutual exchange—give and take happening without strings or expectations—is what sustainable interdependence looks like in action. It's about knowing when to ask for support, when to offer it, and when to step back to reflect or recharge. All these decisions become less about fear and control and more about conscious choice.

Relationships aren't static puzzles to be solved but ever-changing dance partnerships that require tuning in and adjusting constantly. Embracing interdependence asks you to embrace uncertainty. Rather than fearing change or clinging tightly to rigid roles, you learn to flow with what each moment brings. This flexibility nurtures not only your individual wellness but also the health of the partnership. You begin to see your bond not as a chain but as a dynamic thread weaving both your stories together without erasing either one.

It also helps to remember that interdependence doesn't require solving every problem immediately or communicating perfectly all the time. It's more about cultivating a foundation of trust that allows mistakes and misunderstandings to become tools for growth rather than threats to the relationship. When you develop patience and openness as part of your daily practice, you create a safe space where both you and your partner can evolve at your own pace. Growth becomes a shared adventure, not a race or competition.

The lifelong nature of this journey means that your relationship with yourself remains central. You'll find yourself returning often to the practices of self-love, boundary setting, and emotional regulation. These aren't simply skills you use in moments of crisis but habits that become woven into the fabric of your life. The stronger that relationship with your inner self, the more confidently you can show up in all your connections, free from the need to shrink or lose yourself to gain approval or avoid conflict.

It's important to celebrate progress, no matter how small it may seem. Sometimes the advances are subtle—a new way of saying no, an unexpected moment of calm in a triggering situation, or the ability to hold space for your partner's feelings without losing your own footing. Recognizing these wins fuels motivation and reminds you that change is possible and happening, even when it feels slow. Transformation rarely happens overnight; it's the consistent, imperfect efforts accumulated over time that make the difference.

As you embrace this lifelong journey, the community and support you build around you will become invaluable. Whether it's friends, family, therapists, or support groups, having spaces where you're seen, heard, and understood strengthens your resolve and enriches your experience of interdependence. Connection thrives in safety, and cultivating those safe spaces is part of the work you'll be called upon to do repeatedly.

Each step forward also offers an invitation to become an advocate—not just for your own healing but for the cultivation of healthy, interdependent relationships in your wider circles. Sharing your story, encouraging others to explore their own patterns, and helping to dismantle the stigma around emotional interdependence contributes to a culture where healthier connections become the norm, not the exception. Your experience and growth can light the way for others battling their own struggles with codependency.

Ultimately, embracing interdependence as a lifelong journey is about choosing a path of authenticity and courage. There will always be moments of discomfort, uncertainty, and challenge, but within those moments lies the chance to live more fully, love more genuinely, and connect more deeply. It's about honoring your worth, your boundaries, and your capacity to grow alongside the people who matter most.

This journey is not meant to be traveled alone, nor is it a race to a finish line. It is a dance of ongoing discovery, a continuous invitation to show up for yourself and others with empathy and grace. As you embrace interdependence more fully, you cultivate a resilient heart—a heart capable of both independent strength and tender connection, shaping a life rich with meaning, balance, and freedom.

APPENDIX: TOOLS AND RESOURCES FOR CONTINUED GROWTH

As you continue this journey toward healthier, more balanced relationships, having access to the right tools and resources can make all the difference in sustaining your growth. Whether it's thoughtfully chosen books that deepen your understanding, workshops that offer practical experience, or support groups providing compassionate community, these resources are designed to empower you to keep building emotional resilience and boundaries with confidence. Incorporating journaling templates and reflection exercises into your routine can further strengthen self-awareness and help you track your progress without judgment. Remember, lasting change is supported by ongoing learning and connection, so leaning into these aids will help you nurture the strong, interdependent bonds you're working to create and maintain over time.

Recommended Books, Workshops, and Support Groups

One of the most powerful ways to keep growing beyond this book is to continuously seek out resources that resonate with your journey. The path to freedom from unhealthy relationship patterns is rarely a straight line, and having solid tools and a supportive community can make all the difference. Books offer the opportunity to explore ideas deeply at your own pace, while workshops provide immersive experiences for practicing new skills. Support groups, in turn, create spaces where you're not just heard but genuinely understood. Together, these resources can help you sustain progress long after you've closed this book.

When it comes to books, finding the right ones can feel overwhelming. Start with those that have helped countless others untangle the complexities of codependency and build interdependent relationships. Titles that balance practical guidance with compassionate insight allow readers to connect with the material on a personal level. They often combine psychological knowledge with real-life stories, making the concepts relatable and inspiring. Look for works that emphasize healing from childhood wounds, setting boundaries firmly but kindly, and cultivating self-worth without falling into the trap of approval-seeking. Having these books handy means you can revisit key ideas whenever doubts or old patterns resurface.

Workshops, whether in person or online, give you the chance to practice new skills with others who share similar goals. There's something uniquely powerful about stepping out of isolation and into a community space where learning is interactive. Guided sessions on communication skills, emotional regulation, or boundary setting help you make abstract concepts tangible. Plus, facilitators usually offer expert feedback and create safe environments where vulnerability is encouraged, not shamed. Consider workshops that focus on building emotional resilience and healthy intimacy, as those align closely with creating balanced relationships. Some also provide ongoing coaching or follow-up groups, making it easier to maintain momentum and accountability.

Support groups are invaluable because they provide ongoing encouragement and validation. Being around people who truly get what it feels like to struggle with codependency can lift a tremendous weight off your shoulders. These groups often have a shared language, and that deepens connection while reducing feelings of loneliness. Choose groups that promote growth without judgment—spaces where showing vulnerability actually strengthens bonds rather than exposes weakness. Many support groups also incorporate structured formats like Twelve-Step or other recovery models tailored specifically to relationship challenges. Membership in such groups ensures you won't have to face tough moments on your own.

Integrating books, workshops, and support groups creates a robust support system that supports different aspects of your transformation simultaneously. Books feed your mind and spirit at your own pace, workshops flex your interpersonal muscles in structured ways, and support groups meet your need for community and accountability. Together, they form a comprehensive toolkit that supports sustainable change from multiple angles. You might find that a book opens your eyes to a breakthrough concept, a workshop offers the practical tools to apply it, and a support group helps you keep that practice alive during tough days.

Choosing the right set of resources depends a lot on where you are right now on your healing journey. If you're just starting, books can familiarize you with the concepts and language you'll need. As you begin to practice new skills, workshops help solidify those changes through experiential learning. Support groups become essential as you deepen your transformation and encounter setbacks or complex emotions. Remember, growth rarely happens in isolation. It's a dynamic process fueled by learning, practicing, and connecting with others who cheer for your success.

One practical tip for making the most of books is to not rush through them. Take your time, maybe jot down notes or highlight parts that strike a chord. Reflect on how the ideas apply to your own relationship patterns. Some readers benefit from reading aloud or discussing chapters with a trusted friend or therapist. This slows the process and encourages deeper absorption. When attending workshops, come prepared to be open and honest with yourself and others. Growth requires vulnerability, and giving yourself permission to be imperfect in front of others can be freeing.

Participation in support groups is often the biggest challenge for many because it demands ongoing commitment and sometimes confronting uncomfortable emotions. Yet, the rewards are immense. Hearing others' stories can spark hope and help you see that change is possible. Sharing your own experiences with kindness to yourself fosters self-compassion and resilience. These groups remind you that setbacks don't mean failure—they're part of the process. If the first group you try isn't the right fit, keep looking. The right space can feel like coming home.

Importantly, recommended resources should embody the tone and approach that align with your values and needs. Avoid anything that feels too rigid, shaming, or quick-fix oriented. Look for authors and facilitators who honor the complexity of codependency and interdependence without oversimplification. You want guidance that feels hopeful and empowering, not guilt-inducing. Many contemporary authors blend insight from psychology, spirituality, and lived experience in ways that encourage curiosity and growth instead of fear or shame.

Some of the most impactful books are those that also integrate exercises and reflection prompts. These practical elements transform reading from passive into active engagement. You'll find yourself not only understanding concepts but applying them to discover your own truths. When workshops include follow-up materials, recordings, or a community forum, take advantage of those. They extend the learning beyond the scheduled time and deepen skill retention. Support groups that offer recommended reading lists or additional resources often help members build a comprehensive framework for their healing.

Ultimately, the choice of books, workshops, and support groups is an act of self-care and self-investment. Each step you take in seeking out these resources reflects a commitment to growth and freedom. Remember, you're building a foundation that supports you through challenges and opens the door to healthier, more fulfilling relationships. You don't have to do it all at once. Start small. Pick one book to explore, sign up for a local or virtual workshop that fits your schedule, and research a support group nearby or online. Over time, these tools become part of your everyday life—steady companions on the journey to emotional independence and interdependence.

Keeping a journal alongside these resources enhances your progress. Write down insights gained from reading, what you learned in workshops, or reflections after support group meetings. Journaling creates a personal roadmap of your growth and reveals patterns you might otherwise miss. It makes your transformation visible and tangible. Plus, in moments of doubt or discouragement, flipping back through your notes can remind you how far you've come. Pairing reflection with action is a proven way to keep moving forward without feeling stuck.

If you're unsure where to start, many communities and online platforms curate lists of recommended books and vetted workshops based on the latest research and lived experience. These can be excellent shortcuts to high-quality material. Similarly, peer-reviewed support groups often post meeting schedules and descriptions that clarify their focus and approach. Don't hesitate to reach out to facilitators or group leaders with questions about whether a particular resource fits your needs. A willingness to ask and explore models courage and self-respect.

Remember, you are worthy of support and ongoing growth. The work of freeing yourself from codependency and building interdependent relationships takes courage and persistence. The good news is you never have to walk this path alone or without guidance. Books, workshops, and support groups are allies in the transformation process, each offering unique benefits that help you heal, learn, and thrive. Embrace these tools as gifts you give yourself—a commitment to living authentically, lovingly, and with resilience.

Journaling Templates and Reflection Exercises

Journaling can be a powerful tool when it comes to breaking free from unhealthy relationship patterns and moving toward more balanced, interdependent connections. It offers a quiet space where you can explore your thoughts, feelings, and reactions without judgment. Writing regularly allows you to track your progress, uncover hidden emotions, and nurture self-awareness—the foundation of lasting change. Even when progress feels slow or invisible, a committed journaling practice helps illuminate the subtle shifts occurring inside you.

Embedding structured journaling templates into your daily or weekly routine can make this process less overwhelming. Sometimes, knowing where to start is the hardest part. Whether you're new to reflective writing or have journaled before, these guided templates prompt meaningful insight while keeping your reflections focused. They can help you notice recurring patterns, identify triggers, and celebrate small victories that might otherwise go unnoticed. Over time, this habit reinforces a compassionate yet honest self-dialogue that fuels emotional healing.

One common challenge in journaling is avoiding getting stuck in negative loops—focusing too much on what's wrong or what you wish had been different. That's where reflection exercises come into play. These exercises encourage you to shift perspective, explore alternative meanings, and acknowledge growth alongside difficulties. By balancing critical awareness with affirmation of your efforts, reflection encourages patience and resilience. It reminds you that slipping back into old habits is part of the journey, not a sign of failure.

When designing journaling templates for breaking codependency, it's vital to include prompts that touch on both your inner world and how you relate to others. Questions like "What emotions did I notice in my interactions today?" or "Where did I feel triggered or tempted to people-please?" invite you to slow down and observe without self-condemnation. Other prompts might invite you to explore where you exercised healthy boundaries or asked for what you needed—moments of empowerment worth recording. This dual focus on challenges and strengths supports a balanced narrative of growth.

Reflection exercises often work well when paired with gratitude journaling. Noticing the small moments where you felt seen, respected, or connected shifts attention away from scarcity and toward abundance. This doesn't mean ignoring tough experiences, but rather acknowledging that even amidst struggle, relational nourishment exists. Gratitude reinforces that positive emotions and meaningful connections aren't out of reach—which is vital for anyone recovering from codependency, where despair and hopelessness often creep in.

Another helpful journaling approach involves revisiting past entries after some time has passed. This practice can reveal patterns or progress that wasn't obvious in the moment. Looking back a month or two later may show how your thinking evolved, where you built stronger boundaries, or how communication within your relationships has improved. It can also remind you of the setbacks you overcame, reinforcing the idea that healing isn't linear but deeply life-affirming nonetheless.

For those who prefer more variety, creative journaling exercises that go beyond words may also be effective. Drawing your feelings, using metaphors, or crafting dialogues between different parts of yourself can unlock new insights. These forms of expression tap into intuitive knowing and can bypass the mental noise that sometimes clogs traditional journaling. Engaging multiple parts of the brain also helps solidify lessons more deeply, making it easier to translate insights into daily actions.

As you begin or continue your journaling journey, it's important to remember that consistency matters more than perfection. Writing just a few minutes regularly will gradually build your capacity to reflect without judgment. Some days might produce rich entries full of clarity; others might feel sparse or frustrating. Both outcomes carry value. The key is to resist discouragement and keep returning to the practice as an act of self-care and growth.

It's equally beneficial to set an intention before each journaling session. Clarifying what you hope to explore—whether it's understanding a recent argument, recognizing emotional triggers, or celebrating a breakthrough—creates purpose and focus. Intentions keep your reflections rooted in healing rather than rumination, steering your writing toward constructive change.

Besides individual journaling, consider using these templates and reflection exercises as conversation starters with a trusted partner, therapist, or support group. Sharing your discoveries can deepen connection and create accountability. Sometimes articulating your reflections aloud uncovers additional layers of meaning or emotion that written words only hint at. This relational element aligns perfectly with moving toward healthy interdependence, where honest communication and vulnerability are cherished.

To make this practice even more accessible, some templates come with checklists to track daily emotional states or boundary-setting attempts. Others encourage you to rate relationship satisfaction on a scale or note specific actions that felt nourishing versus draining. These structured tools demystify self-reflection, making it concrete and measurable over time. Seeing progress in black-and-white—no matter how small—can renew motivation and reinforce your commitment to change.

When journaling about emotionally charged experiences, it's helpful to adopt a compassionate inner voice. Codependency often arises in the context of self-criticism and fear of abandonment. Writing harshly about yourself only perpetuates old wounds. Instead, speak to yourself as a wise, understanding friend who recognizes effort and growth, even when progress isn't perfect. This gentle tone fosters emotional safety, inviting healing rather than triggering defensiveness or shame.

Importantly, avoid using journaling as a way to hyper-analyze or overthink each interaction. Reflection should spark insight, not paralysis. If you notice yourself spinning into confusion or judgment, it's okay to pause and return to simpler prompts like "What am I grateful for today?" or "What did I do well?" These reset exercises help maintain balance and prevent overwhelm.

Finally, think of journaling templates and reflection exercises as evolving tools—ones you can adapt to your personal journey. As you build emotional resilience and self-trust, some prompts may feel less relevant while new questions arise. Feel free to revise, combine, or create your own templates to meet your current needs and growth areas. This flexibility honors your uniqueness and prevents journaling from becoming a rigid chore.

In sum, journaling and reflection aren't just about writing down feelings or events; they're about cultivating a loving relationship with yourself. Through honest exploration, patience, and acknowledgment of your experiences—both painful and empowering—you lay the groundwork for lasting change. This consistent practice of turning inward strengthens your ability to connect outwardly in healthy, authentic ways. It's one of the most effective tools you can use on your path from codependency to interdependence.

www.ingramcontent.com/pod-product-compliance
Lightning Source LLC
Chambersburg PA
CBHW020350170426
43200CB00005B/118